Cambridge Elements

Elements in International Relations
edited by
Jon C. W. Pevehouse
University of Wisconsin–Madison
Tanja A. Börzel
Freie Universität Berlin
Edward D. Mansfield
University of Pennsylvania

SOCIAL CUES

How the Liberal Community Legitimizes Humanitarian War

Jonathan A. Chu
National University of Singapore

Shaftesbury Road, Cambridge CB2 8EA, United Kingdom

One Liberty Plaza, 20th Floor, New York, NY 10006, USA

477 Williamstown Road, Port Melbourne, VIC 3207, Australia

314–321, 3rd Floor, Plot 3, Splendor Forum, Jasola District Centre, New Delhi – 110025, India

103 Penang Road, #05–06/07, Visioncrest Commercial, Singapore 238467

Cambridge University Press is part of Cambridge University Press & Assessment, a department of the University of Cambridge.

We share the University's mission to contribute to society through the pursuit of education, learning and research at the highest international levels of excellence.

www.cambridge.org
Information on this title: www.cambridge.org/9781009557306

DOI: 10.1017/9781009557276

First published 2025

A catalogue record for this publication is available from the British Library

ISBN 978-1-009-55730-6 Hardback
ISBN 978-1-009-55731-3 Paperback
ISSN 2515-706X (online)
ISSN 2515-7302 (print)

Additional resources for this publication at www.cambridge.org/Chu

Social Cues

How the Liberal Community Legitimizes Humanitarian War

Elements in International Relations

DOI: 10.1017/9781009557276
First published online: February 2025

Jonathan A. Chu
National University of Singapore

Author for correspondence: Jonathan A. Chu, jonchu@nus.edu.sg

Abstract: This Element advances a theory of social cues to explain how international institutions legitimize foreign policy. It reframes legitimization as a type of identity politics. Institutions confer legitimacy by sending social cues that exert pressures to conform and alleviate social–relational concerns regarding norm abidance, group participation, and status and image. Applied to the domain of humanitarian wars, the argument implies that liberal democracies vis-à-vis NATO can influence citizens and policymakers within their community, the primary participants of these military operations. Case studies, news media, a survey of policymakers, and survey experiments conducted in multiple countries validate the social cue theory while refuting alternative arguments relating to legality, material burden sharing, Western regionalism, and rational information transmission. The Element provides an understanding of institutional legitimacy that challenges existing perspectives and contributes to debates about multilateralism, humanitarian intervention, and identity. This title is also available as Open Access on Cambridge Core.

Keywords: international organizations, legitimacy, social identity, public opinion, humanitarian intervention

ISBNs: 9781009557306 (HB), 9781009557313 (PB), 9781009557276 (OC)
ISSNs: 2515-706X (online), 2515-7302 (print)

Contents

1 Institutions and Political Legitimacy, a Debate

Armed humanitarian interventions have emerged as one of the most significant developments in global affairs since the end of the Cold War. These uses of military force, primarily led by democratic countries, pose fundamental questions about how the international community should respond to the worst human atrocities while preserving the principle of state sovereignty. More than that, they also shape and challenge our understanding of the role of liberal values in the international system.[1]

One of the most striking features of humanitarian interventions is their association with multilateral, international institutions.[2] Indeed, political scientist Martha Finnemore argued that since World War II, "to be legitimate, humanitarian interventions must be multilateral."[3] Yet, the precise role these institutions play in legitimizing such actions remains controversial.[4] United Nations Secretary-General Kofi Anan captured this controversy when he articulated the difficult tension facing the UN framework:

> If, in those dark days and hours leading up to the [Rwandan] genocide, a coalition of States had been prepared to act in defense of the Tutsi population, but did not receive prompt Council authorization, should such a coalition have stood aside and allowed the horror to unfold?
>
> To those for whom the Kosovo action heralded a new era when States and groups of States can take military action outside the established mechanisms for enforcing international law, one might ask: Is there not a danger of such interventions undermining the imperfect, yet resilient, security system created after the Second World War, and of setting dangerous precedents for future interventions without a clear criterion to decide who might invoke these precedents, and in what circumstances?[5]

The Security Council, the only institution with the authority to legalize humanitarian intervention, is prone to gridlock. While it is designed to be cautious in authorizing military force and prioritize preventing disputes among the great powers, such a framework could produce severe human costs during a rapidly unfolding humanitarian crisis. On the other hand, turning to alternative multilateral processes, such as NATO's role in the Kosovo crisis, or resorting to unilateralism, poses its own challenges. These alternative approaches risk

[1] Armed or military humanitarian interventions refer to interstate uses of military force to alleviate mass human suffering. They exclude cooperative humanitarian operations in which the target country's legitimate authority invites foreign involvement. Following the legal conventions, these interventions are considered uses of armed force or acts of war. For stylistic reasons, the term will also be used interchangeably with the phrases humanitarian intervention and humanitarian wars.

[2] Schultz 2003. [3] Finnemore 2003. [4] E.g., Caron 1993; Henkin 1999.

[5] Source (accessed November 17, 2023): www.un.org/sg/en/content/sg/speeches/1999-09-20/secretary-general-presents-his-annual-report-general-assembly.

undermining the existing international regime built to safeguard global peace and security and state sovereignty. Moreover, individual governments must also navigate the delicate balance of avoiding domestic and international backlash for conducting foreign policy seen as illegitimate,[6] while simultaneously managing the constraints multilateral institutions impose on their foreign policy autonomy.

These political and human stakes have sparked ongoing debate among policymakers and within public discourse. They also motivate a major body of scholarship on how international institutions influence the political legitimacy of foreign policies, including humanitarian intervention.[7] In fact, since Claude Inis observed that the United Nations could generate "legitimacy," scholars have spent decades unpacking what that truly means.[8] Given Realist theory's strong presumption that institutions have little impact on international security and war, researchers have grappled with why these seemingly powerless bodies hold any significance. Why does international support for a country's foreign policy grow when such a policy receives institutional approval? If institutions do matter, which ones can bestow legitimacy, and why?[9]

At least three lines of research address these questions. First, Constructivist scholars argue that an institution's power to legitimize comes from its ability to shape beliefs about what behavior is appropriate and what *ought* to be followed. When a policy, such as military intervention, receives institutional legitimacy, it gains wider acceptance and support. Endorsements from multilateral institutions, for example, can reveal broad, international approval and that the purpose of intervention is not merely self-serving.[10] These institutions could also confer legitimacy by producing favorable and fair outcomes and by following appropriate procedures.[11] Conversely, the absence of institutional backing can also delegitimize a country's foreign policy.[12] These pathways to legitimacy are rooted in the social interactions between political actors and institutions.

[6] On the potential cost of international backlash in terms of soft power, see Nye 2004; Pape 2005; Goldsmith and Horiuchi 2009; Goldsmith and Horiuchi 2012.

[7] By political legitimacy, I refer to whether people, including citizens and elites, perceive political behavior to be legitimate. This contrasts with legitimacy in the theoretical, normative sense. In the remainder of this Element, I drop the political from political legitimacy.

[8] Claude 1967, Chapter 4. A related question asks why people see institutions themselves as legitimate (e.g., Dellmuth and Tallberg 2015).

[9] This Element does not evaluate the separate question of whether humanitarian intervention "works."

[10] Finnemore 2003, 82.

[11] This argument is applied to the Security Council in particular (Hurd 2008, 67–73). More broadly, legitimacy by IOs can be granted when they reflect commonly accepted rules (Coleman 2007).

[12] Finnemore 2003.

A second line of research argues that institutions legitimize the use of armed force by legalizing it.[13] People may be more inclined to support legally sanctioned actions due to their intrinsic respect for the rule of law in the international system.[14] Legality can also hold practical value. For instance, adhering to international law helps safeguard a country's reputation.[15] From this perspective, because the Security Council holds the exclusive authority under the current international legal system to authorize military action outside of self-defense,[16] it should have a unique ability to legitimize uses of armed force, including humanitarian interventions.

A third line of research recasts the concept of legitimization in rational, game-theoretic terms, leading to what is broadly known as rational information transmission theories. One study posits that the Security Council's endorsements act as signals that reassure observers about the potential for military force to provoke great power conflict and destabilize the international system.[17] A subsequent body of research emphasizes how institutions can convey information that shifts public perceptions about the motives behind war and its potential material cost and benefits.[18] To explain *why* institutions can send such signals, these theories focus on institutional characteristics such as independence (neutrality) and conservativeness.[19] Independent institutions include a diverse range of veto players, and conservative institutions set a high bar for policy approval. Overall, these arguments generally suggest that policy endorsements by the Security Council are influential because they represent an elite pact, a diverse group of countries, and a significant barrier to authorizing military action.

This arc of scholarship has profoundly influenced international relations theory. It has taken the field from a general skepticism about the relevance of international institutions to what is now the conventional wisdom: the Security Council and other institutions enable governments to reassure, signal, and ultimately persuade skeptical audiences, including the mass public and foreign elites, about the legality and merits of their foreign policy.[20]

13 Tago 2005, 589; Tago and Ikeda 2015, 392.

14 Chong 1993; Koh 1997; Finnemore and Sikkink 1998; Goodman and Jinks 2013; Hafner-Burton et al. 2016.

15 Guzman 2008; Tomz 2008. 16 Frank 2002. 17 Voeten 2005.

18 Fang 2008; Thompson 2009; Chapman 2011.

19 Claude (1967, 114) makes a similar point in discussing how the UN's legitimacy could emerge from its Switzerland-like neutrality.

20 Researchers also provide insights into how information signaling works in the international political economy. Gray (2009), for example, shows how the European Union signals information about risk and a country's economic performance. See also, Brutger and Li (2002) and Gray and Hicks (2014).

However, some puzzling cases and recent research highlight the need for additional theorizing and empirical investigation to better grasp these institutional dynamics. For instance, the historical record includes cases where international institutions other than the Security Council conferred legitimacy. In 1999, the United States and NATO allies conducted an armed humanitarian intervention in Kosovo without Security Council approval. But rather than condemning the United States, much of the international community declared that the illegal intervention was nevertheless legitimate.[21] Even several non-Western members of the Security Council refrained from condemning the intervention.[22] Theories focusing on international law struggle to explain these events. Similarly, existing information models emphasizing institutional traits like independence and neutrality fall short of explaining NATO's apparent ability to legitimize intervention. After all, NATO is often seen as a homogenous body with a reputation for aligning with U.S. interests.

Recent experimental research also reveals intriguing patterns existing theories cannot fully explain. One study found that governments can raise support for their policies among foreign public simply by seeking Security Council approval, even if that approval is ultimately denied due to opposition from some of the permanent (P5) council members.[23] This finding suggests that neither legality nor an explicit endorsement from the great powers is required for an institution to have influence. It also underscores public skepticism of the Security Council's procedural element, particularly the P5's "veto" power. Meanwhile, existing studies show that institutional approval does not necessarily lead people to reassess their beliefs about the material costs and benefits of war,[24] and that IOs other than the Security Council can rally support for war in ways that existing models cannot account for.[25] In sum, while current research demonstrates the ability of international institutions to influence politics by shaping domestic and international opinion, there is a clear theoretical gap in understanding *why* this influence exists and *which* institutions can wield it.

1.1 Interpreting Legitimization as a Social Cue

This Element develops a new theory to understand how international institutions shape the perceived legitimacy of foreign policy. It advances a social theory of legitimacy that builds upon political psychology, social identity theory, as well as insights about state-level norms from constructivist literature. It begins with the premise that legitimacy is in the eye of the beholder, so to

[21] Independent International Commission on Kosovo 2000.
[22] Source (accessed November 10, 2023): https://press.un.org/en/1999/19990326.sc6659.html.
[23] Tago and Ikeda 2015. [24] Tingley and Tomz 2012.
[25] E.g., Recchia and Chu 2022; Kertzer 2023.

theorize and uncover evidence about it, one must first begin with the audience of legitimacy: individuals.

To preview, Section 2 elucidates the social cue theory in two main parts. It first explains how social cues work in general terms to lay down the theory's underlying logic, allowing researchers to apply it to other phenomena. It then develops the theory in the specific context of humanitarian intervention by the community of liberal democracies. Generally stated, the theory interprets legitimization as a social process driven by identity. It argues that institutions, depending on the identities they represent, confer legitimacy by sending social cues about whether a policy is socially appropriate and how a specific group of countries will receive it. These cues operate through *relational mechanisms*, alleviating concerns about norm abidance, group participation, as well as status and image, and by exerting *direct social pressure* on group members to conform. Additionally, the theory explains how individuals and communities of ingroup members both can send social cues, but that those cues are more influential when channeled through institutions. When an institution represents a social group, it can amplify and clarify the social meaning of a cue, enhancing its legitimizing effect.

By analyzing institutional legitimization in terms of identity politics, the social cue theory produces a new set of propositions regarding whose cues matter and why. Cues from ingroup members or institutions should matter most because they exert social pressure and induce social considerations regarding a policy. In the case of humanitarian interventions, the relevant ingroup is the community of liberal democracies, which are the main actors behind these interventions, and its closely linked institution, NATO. The theory implies that liberal democracies vis-à-vis NATO can send social cues to influence how domestic and foreign community members perceive humanitarian intervention. This phenomenon occurs because these audiences view NATO as an international organization (IO)[26] representing their ingroup.[27] In contrast, cues from outgroup countries and institutions representing a more diffuse community like the Security Council exert less social influence, particularly when an ingroup cue already exists. Section 2 concludes with a discussion of alternative explanations (regarding material considerations and Western regionalism), scope conditions (relating to policy domain, temporality, and political actors), and how the social cue theory is distinct from existing informational arguments.

[26] IOs are a type of formal international institution that include sovereign governments as their members. This manuscript refers to NATO, the UN, and other IOs as international institutions and IOs interchangeably.

[27] This perception may or may not be based on hypocrisy or illusion, which exists in all types of social groups, from religious to political organizations.

Sections 3–5 test the social cue theory's implications through a multi-method research design, using historical polls, case studies of U.S. intervention, news media analysis, a survey of policymakers in the United Kingdom, and nine public opinion surveys and survey experiments conducted in the United States, Japan, and Egypt. The findings from these studies support the social cue theory while refuting alternative explanations.

To begin, during humanitarian interventions, both the Security Council and NATO are highly visible to citizens in liberal democracies – appearing in news articles, speeches, and media broadcasts. As a result, their policy positions become key social cues to the public.

Next, the historical record of U.S. intervention and original survey experiments reveal that ingroup cues significantly influence domestic public opinion. Americans tend to be skeptical of interventions without institutional backing, such as in the case of Rwanda and Syria. They are more enthusiastic about intervention when formal institutional backing is involved but express little distinction between NATO's sole approval versus both NATO and the Security Council's backing. Thus, the historical data suggest that ingroup cues from NATO and the liberal community raise domestic public approval, while the Security Council's additional endorsement has minimal impact. Moreover, survey experiments demonstrate the causality found in the historical record. NATO's policy endorsements cause an increase in public support for intervention. Furthermore, once an ingroup cue from NATO is sent, the Security Council does little to shift public opinion. The reverse, however, is not true. Even with a Security Council endorsement, NATO's additional endorsement still increases public approval. Lastly, the experiments also show that social cues from the liberal community influence public opinion, but its cues exert an even stronger influence when conveyed through NATO, demonstrating the power of institutionalized social cues.

Three additional empirical results demonstrate the social cue theory's causal processes while ruling out alternative explanations relating to military and material burden-sharing capacity. First, NATO's influence is most substantial among individuals who associate NATO with the liberal community and who express affinity with its member countries, rather than those who associate NATO solely with military strength. Second, NATO's impact on public opinion operates through the theorized relational mechanisms: concerns about norm abidance, group participation, and status and image. Third, even after removing its ability to change people's cost-benefit calculations, NATO continues to shape public support for military intervention.

Social cues influence the foreign audiences of an intervening country as well. Analysis of news articles, historical polls, and original survey experiments shows that NATO and the liberal community's cues similarly affect Japanese support for U.S. humanitarian interventions, just as they do in the U.S. domestic context. These results contribute to debates about American soft power and challenge the notion that NATO's influence is limited to the West. Turning to foreign elites, a representative survey of UK parliamentarians reveals that they prefer humanitarian intervention with NATO but without the Security Council's approval over the reverse. In contrast, neither NATO nor the Security Council significantly affects Egyptian public opinion, which instead is more strongly influenced by the Arab League. These findings are consistent with the social cue theory, reinforcing the importance of ingroup cues. Taken together, the evidence shows that the liberal community and NATO can legitimize humanitarian wars by sending powerful social cues to domestic and international audiences.

The final two sections revisit the existing literature on how international institutions affect domestic and foreign opinion on war, demonstrating this Element's broader contributions to the field of international relations. Section 6 reinterprets existing studies on international law and rational information transmission, showing that evidence previously seen as consistent with legal or material theories can be explained through the lens of social cues. The section also presents additional analysis to test more specific claims made by the existing theories, focusing on political knowledge. These analyses ultimately uncover empirical patterns that can only be explained by the social cue theory. Section 7 discusses the academic and policy implications of the Element. It explains how the Element advances our understanding of legitimacy, forum shopping,[28] and the role of identity in international relations, and concludes by contemplating practical questions about humanitarian wars led by the democratic community.

2 A Theory of Social Cues

This section develops a novel theory of social cues to explain how political communities and international institutions legitimize, and thereby influence, people's perceptions of armed humanitarian intervention. Legitimization is understood here as a social process in which some stimulus leads people to conform to their social group and view a particular behavior or opinion as consistent with their identity. The theory proceeds in two subsections: first, as a *general argument* on how social groups send institutionalized social cues; and second, as a *specific application* on how IOs influence humanitarian wars by the liberal democratic community in the post–Cold War era. The section subsequently examines alternative explanations, questions of generalizability, and how the social cue theory distinguishes itself from rational informational

[28] E.g., Voeten 2001; Lipscy 2017.

theories. The section concludes by outlining the findings presented in the subsequent evidentiary sections.

2.1 The General Argument

The social cue theory begins with premises rooted in social and political psychology, including social identity theory (SIT), but innovates theoretically to advance a new framework for understanding how institutions convey social cues. People develop social identities when they identify with a particular group. These social groups can form around ascriptive attributes like age, race, and gender as well as ideologies, hobbies, professions, and other qualities. Identification with a group creates a sense of belonging, distinguishing "us" from "them." This "ingroup-outgroup" distinction shapes people's understanding of their social world, a concept central to SIT. Scholars of international relations similarly highlight how group identification and ideology foster inclusion, exclusion, and relational comparisons, influencing behavior and preferences in international affairs.[29]

Identifying with a group also means acquiring a stake in the group's collective well-being and adopting the group's perspective. For example, individuals may feel pride based on the performance of their sports team, ethnicity, or country. This phenomenon involves developing a sense of social self or collective social identity,[30] which leads people to experience "collective self-esteem" and emotions based on their group's experiences.[31] Collective identification also leads people to make intergroup comparisons (which contrasts with comparisons between self and others at the individual level).[32] They will care about how their group interacts and relates to other groups.

This concept of collective identity is central to international relations scholarship, which shows how the social belonging of countries, governments, and their citizens influence their preferences and behavior in international affairs.[33] For example, German citizens adopting their national identity may think about the world from the perspective of their country, Germany, as a social actor in international politics. Research in international relations also emphasizes how social identities can transfer from country to individual: if countries belong to a larger social group, then that country's citizens will also tend to perceive themselves as belonging to such a group. For example, Germany is a part of Europe, so to some degree, Germans share

[29] E.g., Abdelal et al. 2009, 20–24; Allan, Vucetic, and Hopf 2018, 849. IR scholarship draws from sociological and constructivist traditions, in addition to social identity theory from social psychology.

[30] Brewer and Gardner 1996.

[31] Crocker and Luhtanen 1990; Branscombe and Wann 1994.

[32] Brewer and Gardner 1996.

[33] Mercer 1995; Wendt 1999; Johnston 2008.

a collective European identity.[34] Overall, countries and their citizens can develop ingroup identities based on economic, political, social, and other factors, in addition to geography.

Extensive research documents how people's identities affect their opinions, decisions, and behavior both as individuals within a group and as someone who has internalized their group's collective identity. One of the most consistent findings in this area is ingroup favoritism, the tendency to favor those within one's identity group. This favoritism can be observed in a wide range of actions, from essential services like providing health care to smaller acts of assistance like helping a stranger who has dropped their groceries.[35] In international relations, this tendency influences humanitarian aid, where individuals are more inclined to help foreigners sharing their racial or religious background.[36] A notable example arose during the Russian invasion of Ukraine, where a shared European identity contributed to widespread receptivity toward Ukrainian refugees[37] – a response that contrasted with the more limited support for Syrian refugees fleeing conflict.[38] Ultimately, ingroup favoritism is a well-documented phenomenon influencing various aspects of social, economic, and political interactions globally.

Beyond ingroup favoritism, people identifying with a group are more likely to adhere to its views and behave consistently with its norms and practices. This tendency, in part, is driven by self-esteem: people seek to feel good about themselves, and they often adopt their group's standards as a measure of self-worth and status. For instance, academics are socialized to feel validated by publishing in particular research journals or achieving specific career milestones. From a more rationalist perspective, people's incentive to affirm their identities can be interpreted as an "identity-based payoff," where people gain satisfaction from the identity-affirming actions of themselves and others.[39] Individuals might also follow their group's behavior and norms for less calculated and more instinctual reasons, out of habit, emulation, and herd mentality. This can include a natural aversion to standing out or appearing deviant within a group to which they feel deeply connected. In this way, both calculated and subconscious motivations contribute to individuals' alignment with their group's values and practices.

Following this line of thought, I argue that social cues influence people's opinions and behavior by operating on their desire to conform to and affirm their

[34] For a discussion of multiple, overlapping, and nested identities, see Risse 2011.

[35] E.g., Hall et al. 2015; Choi et al. 2022. [36] Chu and Lee 2024. [37] Politi et al. 2023.

[38] See, for example (accessed November 11, 2024): www.cbc.ca/news/world/europe-racism-ukraine-refugees-1.6367932.

[39] Akerlof and Kranton 2000.

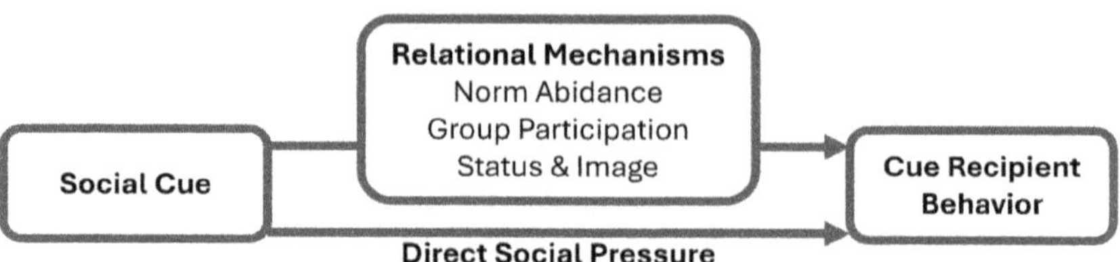

Figure 1 Conceptual schema of social cues. Social cues channel their influence through social-relational mechanisms and by exerting direct social pressures to conform.

identities. The dynamic of social cueing occurs when a "sender" sends a cue to a "recipient," and the recipient perceives the sender as belonging to its social group. The transmission of a social cue could be direct or indirect. For example, a sender could relay its opinion directly to a recipient, or a sender can publicly declare its opinion on a matter while the recipient observes that declaration. Cues include statements or actions that endorse a point of view, type of behavior, or policy. However, they do not rely on imposing a direct material cost or benefit on a recipient's behavior, distinguishing them from coercive threats or inducement.

These social cues influence people through two main channels, illustrated in Figure 1. The first channel involves *relational mechanisms*, which tap into the following three key preferences stemming from people's social identity. Preference number one is *norm abidance*, or people's desire to behave consistently with their group's norms and practices and advance their group's values and goals, rather than those of an outgroup.[40] They may find intrinsic value in upholding the group's values, while they also may fear social disapproval for violating group norms or going against their peers. This adherence can reflect a commitment to a specific norm or a broader, more intangible desire to do what is "right" or "appropriate." For instance, a Christian may strive to uphold specific norms around charity, marriage, and the family, or more generally, seek to embody what it means to be a "good" Christian. In this sense, social cues push individuals to behave consistently with their group's values.

Preference number two is *group participation*, or people's desire to be part of their group's activities. People often prefer to do things alongside their peers, whether going out for a movie or engaging in a multilateral foreign policy. On the other hand, people may also have a "fear of missing out" when they are left out of the activities of their social group. Social cues thus induce this desire to be part of the community.

[40] See especially Duque's (2018) concept of social closure.

Preference number three is *status and image*, or people's desire to maintain a high status and a good image among their peers. For many, maintaining a good image serves not only as an intrinsic source of self-esteem but also as an instrumental way to secure a sense of high status within a group.[41] This desire can lead to social ladder-climbing behaviors as well, as individuals seek recognition and approval. Furthermore, this drive for status and a positive image often extends beyond the individual to the group as a whole: people want their group to be respected within an even larger, superordinate community. For instance, a tennis player may want to be well-regarded among her fellow players while desiring that tennis itself to be well-regarded relative to other sports. Thus, social cues act upon these concerns about status and image, which in turn influence people's opinions and behaviors. Together, these three mechanisms – norm abidance, group participation, and status/image – help to explain how social cues influence people's opinions and behaviors.[42]

The second channel of social cues operates more directly, affecting individuals through *direct social pressure*. In this case, social cues prompt recipients to adopt certain beliefs or behaviors without explicit reward, punishment, or incentive. Instead, recipients change their opinions or behavior through an almost automatic or instinctual process of emulation, mimicking, and conformity. This direct pressure might be described as a "normative nudge," and there is no intervening mechanism in its causal pathway. In summary, social cues play a dual role of social influence: they ameliorate social-relational concerns, while also directly socializing group members into conformity.[43] From the surface, this dual role can be interpreted as conferring legitimacy on a point of view or behavior among a particular social group.

Who or what types of entities can send social cues? The sender of these cues can be individuals, groups of individuals, or formal bodies or organizations. Among these, cues from ingroup members exert the strongest influence. Indeed, experimental research shows that people update their beliefs and change their behavior after gleaning information from fellow group members.[44] Other

---

[41] While status can draw from attributes such as wealth and military might, I conceptualize status as a social-relational concept, following Weber (1978); Duquc (2018). Renshon (2017) focuses on status as a positional concept or maker of hierarchy.

[42] While distinct, these three behaviors are also interrelated and mutually reinforcing. For example, participating in group activities and being seen as abiding by community norms are ways to maintain status and a good image.

[43] Here, the term social influence is used more broadly than in Johnston (2008), which defines the concept as "a class of microprocesses that elicit pro-normative behavior through the distribution of social rewards and punishments." Johnston's definition focuses on the cost and benefits element, while I additionally consider direct social pressure that elicits conformity.

[44] Gershon and Fridman (2022), Study 5.

studies show that cues from the like-minded can influence people's trade attitudes.[45] Yet other research finds that cues from social peers can influence public opinion as strongly as those from political elites.[46] Within a group, cues from veteran or high-status members tend to be more influential than those from novices.[47] By contrast, cues from outgroup members are generally discounted or even met with resistance, especially when the outgroup is perceived negatively or is socially distant.[48]

Social cues are particularly impactful when they are institutionalized. In international relations, for example, international organizations (IOs) can institutionalize the cues sent by certain countries or groups of countries. In this context, institutionalization designates a cue-sender as representing a particular social group using rules, titles, or formal organizations. Furthermore, such a designation can elevate the status of a cue-sender within their community. For example, a religious leader with a specific title can send cues about the social implications of various behaviors for members of a particular religion. The role of a religious leader is institutionalized (e.g., a church pastor or an abbot of a temple), which places them in a better position than other ingroup members to send social cues about what constitutes identity-congruent behavior. To provide another example, the European Union and its high commissioner are formal institutions that could effectively send social cues to the community of European states and citizens, compared to other ingroup members like the German government or some high official that happens to be European.

Institutions, when recognized as representing a social group, can amplify the impact of a social cue in two related ways. First, institutionalization clarifies the social meaning of a cue. Individuals, countries, and other entities often have multiple identities, so a cue's social meaning may be ambiguous to observers. Take, for example, a pastor named Mike, who is also a parent, political party member, and engineer. If Mike, dressed in everyday clothes, shares a political opinion at a town hall meeting, fellow religious group members might be unsure whether to interpret his views through a religious lens or as influenced by his other roles. However, if he expresses the same views from the pulpit, members of his religious community are likely to interpret and respond to his statement within the context of their shared faith and identity.

Second, institutions can play a "logistical" role by coordinating group decision-making and facilitating the delivery of a social cue to group members. Even if individuals (or states) share an identity, they may have difficulty

[45] Brutger and Li (2022). [46] Kerzter and Zeitzoff (2017). [47] Johnston (2001, 2008).

[48] Empirical research on social identity theory finds that ingroup affinity does not consistently translate into outgroup animus, including in international relations (e.g., Ko 2022, 2023; Chu and Lee 2024).

agreeing on a group's goals, agenda, and actions. And even if they are aligned, they may struggle to effectively communicate their views to the broader group, especially if the group is large or dispersed. Institutions address these challenges by facilitating group decision-making and promoting communication through channels like traditional and internet media, mailing lists, and gatherings, enhancing the visibility and reach of its viewpoints. So, overall, social cues sent through institutions representing an identity group are likely to have greater reach and provide clearer guidance on ingroup norms.

To summarize, the social cue theory argues that people are more likely to support policies and engage in behavior endorsed by their social group while discounting the opinions of outgroup members. These endorsements, or social cues, influence ingroup behavior both directly – through a "normative nudge" effect that encourages emulation and conformity – and indirectly by mitigating relational concerns about norm abidance, group participation, and status and image. Social cues are particularly strong when delivered through institutionalized channels, such as formal organizations representing the group. This process of social cueing ultimately serves to legitimize certain behaviors and viewpoints for group members.

Before turning to the issue of humanitarian intervention, it is crucial to elaborate on the social cue theory's main requirements. For social cues to work, cue recipients need to identify with the social group of the cue sender, but only to a minimal degree. Namely, cue recipients need only have some sense, whether explicitly or subconsciously, that they belong to the group. This standard most closely aligns with SIT, particularly from the minimal group paradigm tradition.[49] From this perspective, even trivial things like being sorted into the blue or red group can be the basis of group identity,[50] though if the identity marker is too trivial, it may not be a stable and long-lasting identity. Similarly, for *institutionalized* social cues to work, ingroup members need to have some sense, whether explicitly or subconsciously, that the institution is associated with their social group.

Two important points follow. First, members of a social group can still be susceptible to social cues even if they lack detailed knowledge of their group's norms. For example, a person may consider themselves a member of the U.S. Republican Party. Similarly, someone who identifies as Christian may not be familiar with all the ways their beliefs and actions align (or don't) with their faith. However, both of these individuals would still be susceptible to social

[49] E.g., Tajfel 1978, 1981; Tajfel and Turner 1986.

[50] Constructivists, in contrast, often theorize about identity and social community as a "thicker" concept, entailing holding a set of intersubjective beliefs and values and engaging in group behaviors (e.g., Risse 2011).

cues by their group. Second, a social group can form around a certain set of values but abandon those values over time while still waving the group's banner. This phenomenon could lead to organized hypocrisy in identity politics. Thus, one can identify with a social group and be susceptible to its social cues without necessarily understanding, internalizing, or keeping pace with its evolving values and practices.

2.2 Social Cues by the Liberal Community and NATO

In three parts, I will now apply the general formulation of the social cue theory to international politics and, specifically, to understanding how international institutions legitimize and, therefore, influence the domestic politics of humanitarian wars waged by liberal democracies. This discussion will generate a series of hypotheses regarding how the Security Council, NATO, and their member governments affect people's views on humanitarian intervention, which will be tested in the subsequent empirical sections.

The first part of the argument establishes the liberal democratic community and NATO as the social group and institution most central to the phenomenon of armed humanitarian interventions. The United States, along with other liberal democracies, is the primary participant of humanitarian interventions, and substantial research on political communities suggests that these countries are embedded in a broader social grouping of democratic countries. This democratic community distinguishes itself from outgroup countries governed by authoritarian regimes, closed economic systems, and those with limited fundamental rights.[51] This us versus them perspective was undoubtedly promoted during the Cold War, with both sides framing the world as ideologically divided between good and bad systems.[52] While such a perspective may have been elite-driven and motivated by material interest, the notion that democracies share an identity gained traction and continued to shape foreign policy and identity even after the fall of the Berlin Wall.[53] This democratic identity also influences how various political actors, including the public, perceive which states are "friends" or "foes."[54] Indeed, reflecting on the resilience of political identities, Peter Katzenstein noted that political actors "attribute far deeper meanings to the

[51] E.g., Deutsch et al. 1957; Risse-Kappen 1996.

[52] But even earlier, political thinkers from Immanuel Kant to Thomas Paine wrote about the special relation among representative governments.

[53] E.g., Gheciu 2005. More generally, see Snyder (1991) for an incisive argument on how norms and ideas embedded in top-down elite rhetoric and "myths" could take root in domestic society, develop a life of their own, and subsequently affect policy from the bottom up. This Element, however, focuses on testing the implications of democratic community on social cueing rather than tracing the formation of the community.

[54] E.g., Chu 2021.

historical battles that define collective identities than to the transient conflicts of daily politics."[55]

Beyond representing a distinct social group, the liberal community is defined by a shared set of norms and practices.[56] Members follow a "logic of appropriateness," or a set of beliefs about how they should behave,[57] which may be formally codified or informally accepted and adhered to as part of a "community of practice."[58] For liberal democracies, this means governments and their citizens alike tend to avoid coercive bargaining or violence in interstate relations, although this courtesy may not extend to interactions with outgroup nations.[59] Relevant to this study, these democracies also uphold norms of consultation, emphasizing the need for collective deliberation with other democratic states in foreign policy.[60] As a result, democracies often take the policy endorsements of other group members into serious consideration.[61]

Other research demonstrates how the social distinction between democracies and non-democracies influences international politics. On a macro level, democratic ideological and normative group distinctions affect which states wage war with one another,[62] form military alliances,[63] and perceive other governments as threats.[64] An analysis of UN General Assembly voting records even reveals that commitments to liberalism create a coherent "liberal order" grouping in international affairs.[65]

Group behavior among countries – whether it be the deliberation of policy or conduct of joint operations – often occurs within a multilateral IO. When it comes to the democratic community, a long tradition of scholarship observes that NATO is emblematic of this group of countries, particularly in contrast to other IOs like the Security Council.[66] This line of research, often traced back to Karl Deutsch and colleagues' seminal 1957 study of the North Atlantic community, links NATO's role its member countries' commitment to shared norms

---

[55] Katzenstein 1996a, 3. [56] Katzenstein 1996b; Adler 1997; Wendt 1999.

[57] March and Olsen 1998. [58] Adler 2008.

[59] I.e., the democratic peace. See Doyle 1986; Maoz and Russett 1993; Tomz and Weeks 2013.

[60] Risse-Kappen 1995; Adler 2008, 204–206.

[61] I do not take a stance on whether this is due to habit, practice, or norms.

[62] Doyle 1986; Maoz and Russett 1993. [63] Lai and Reiter 2000. [64] Risse-Kappen 1995.

[65] Bailey, Strezhnev, and Voeten 2017.

[66] This general observation does not deny exceptions like the autocratic Turkey in NATO. The existence of deviants does not negate the existence of an entire group. Furthermore, this argument does not claim that NATO's *initial* formation was necessarily caused by shared identity: See Rathbun (2011, Chapter 5) for a discussion of the structural-realist conventional wisdom and a new argument about how the domestic politics of generalized trust played a role in the formation of NATO. Also, note how the social theory could complement Rathbun's notion of generalized trust. It could be the case that mass support for IOs could be a result of generalized trust, but it could also be the case that such trust is contingent on social group identification, so it is strongest for ingroup members.

and values.[67] Subsequent research shows how NATO's function as a political community of norms and values further sheds light on its operational practices, institutional survival,[68] as well as how its members maintain peace and engage in conflict.[69] NATO's expansion into Eastern Europe can be understood in terms of social identity community building by liberal democracies as well.[70] Thus, while the democratic community exists as a group of countries, NATO has become a key institution embodying its social identity and place in international relations.

To be clear, understanding NATO as a social community does not negate its role as a military alliance. These functions are not mutually exclusive and may even be complementary. In fact, even NATO itself recognizes its dual mission of providing security and advancing democratic norms and group cohesion. Since the end of the Cold War, NATO has explicitly placed promoting and defending liberal democratic values and community on par with its security mandate. This is evident in NATO's Strategic Concept documents, which serve as its primary public statements that articulate its purpose, principles, and goals. The early Strategic Concepts (1950–1968) emphasized NATO's strength as a military alliance, though they still acknowledged its interest in safeguarding democracy. Beginning with the fifth Strategic Concept in 1990, however, NATO has increasingly emphasized its social role in building and embodying a "shared community" of democratic values. The 2022 Strategic Concept, for example, states on its first page:

> We remain steadfast in our resolve to protect our one billion citizens, defend our territory and safeguard our freedom and democracy. We will reinforce our unity, cohesion and solidarity, building on the enduring transatlantic bond between our nations and the strength of our shared democratic values. We reiterate our steadfast commitment to the North Atlantic Treaty and to defending each other from all threats, no matter where they stem from.

This statement underscores NATO's dual identity, reflecting its mission to uphold both democratic ideals and military security.[71]

In sum, NATO can be understood as an ingroup IO for democratic nations.[72] In contrast, the Security Council has a more diffuse and less defined social

---

[67] Deutsch et al. 1957. [68] Risse-Kappen 1996; Schimmelfennig 2003; Adler 2008.

[69] Adler and Barnett 1998. [70] Shimmelfennig 2003.

[71] Whether or not these proclamations are hypocrisy are beside the point of assessing whether citizens in the democratic community have come to believe NATO to hold such an identity.

[72] Note that the theory only requires members of the democratic community to *perceive* NATO as representing their ingroup in international relations. This perception may or may not be built on hypocrisy or illusion. To draw an analogy, there have been religious organizations motivated and sustained by impure or hypocritical reasons, but that does not change the fact that their members

identity, which, according to social cue theory, limits the influence of its cues. While the Security Council includes some democratic members, it also represents a range of nondemocratic states and thus reflects a broader range of the international community. Indeed, a defining feature of the Security Council is its heterogeneous membership.[73] If it exclusively represented nondemocratic governments, it might convey an outgroup social cue, but as it stands, it occupies an ambiguous position in terms of ideological and social alignment with the democratic community.

The second part of the argument turns to the micro-level and assesses how the democratic community and NATO's representation of it manifests within individuals. For the social cues to influence attitudes toward humanitarian interventions, a meaningful segment of people within democratic countries must identify, at least loosely, with the broader liberal community. According to the social cue theory, individuals need only a minimal or "thin" identification with a group for such cues to take effect. Often, people associate with a group before internalizing all the group's values. This means that not all members of the liberal community will necessarily understand or strictly adhere to its norms, practices, and ideals. Rather, it is enough that people feel, even if just implicitly, that other liberal democracies and NATO are "on the same team" and constitute their ingroup. By holding this basic degree of identification, individuals become susceptible to social cues, though a stronger group identification may amplify these effects. This section supports the plausibility of these assumptions regarding people's identity attachments.

A substantial body of research theorizes and documents how identities in international relations manifest at the individual and mass public levels.[74] Within the liberal community, people's values and identification with other democracies are shaped by elite communication, news media, education, and public discourse.[75] Studies show that democracy and its values affect both mass public and policymaker attitudes toward international affairs.[76] For example, research from the transpacific region shows that democratic leaders' appeals to shared liberal values affect citizen attitudes toward military alliances.[77] Relatedly, global opinions about China's rise as a superpower vary significantly based on people's democratic orientation, even when controlling for national security and economic interests.[78]

perceive group belonging. For a debate over whether NATO's survival should be understood in terms of democracy or not, see Thies (2009) and Sayle (2019).

[73] Thompson 2009. [74] E.g., Risse 2011; Bayram 2015. [75] Allan, Vucetic, and Hopf 2018.

[76] Herrmann and Shannon 2001; Johns and Davies 2012; Lacina and Lee 2013; Tomz and Weeks 2013, 2020.

[77] Chu, Ko, and Liu 2021. [78] Chu 2021.

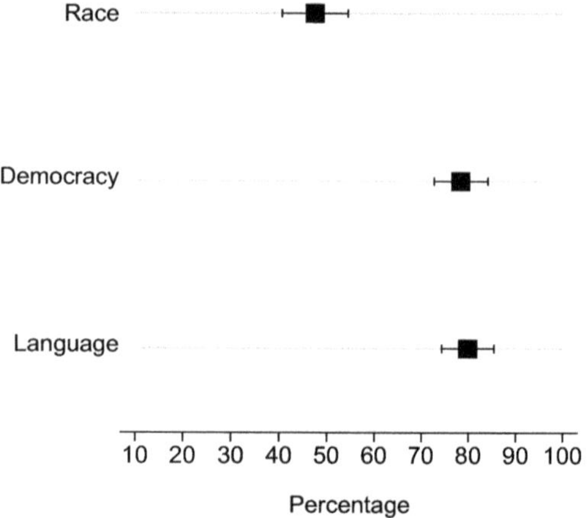

Figure 2 Americans can better relate to foreigners from democratic systems. Question asked, "What allows people from different countries to relate with one another?" The percentages capture those who responded somewhat, very, or extremely important, as opposed to not very or not at all important. $N = 704$. Survey USA-5.

Corroborating these findings, Figure 2 presents data from a survey of Americans and shows that about 78 percent of the respondents believed that sharing a political system was at least "Somewhat Important" in determining whether citizens of different countries could relate to one another. Eighty percent saw language, a key marker of shared identity, as important.[79] In contrast, only about 45 percent considered race an important basis for international relations.

Additional research documents how NATO membership affects public beliefs and values related to liberal democracy. For example, after joining NATO, countries like the Czech Republic and Romania adopted textbooks and implemented educational campaigns that promoted democratic frames of thinking, prompting citizens and elites to prioritize and see liberal values and human rights as legitimate.[80] This experience reflects a broader pattern of liberal democratic community-building in Eastern Europe, where NATO has served as a socializing force, fostering identification with democratic norms and values.[81]

More recent examples from NATO's public diplomacy provide additional evidence of how it fosters a collective identity among individuals. NATO states, as a core tenet, that it "promotes democratic values and enables members to consult and cooperate on defense and security-related issues."[82] To this end,

[79] Laitin 1998. [80] Gheciu 2005. [81] Shimmelfennig 2003.
[82] Source (accessed November 10, 2024): www.nato.int/nato-welcome/.

NATO and its affiliates often portray the alliance as a value-driven, group-oriented community. For instance, in June 2017, NATO tweeted, "We are an Alliance of like-minded countries ... We are united ... #WeAreNATO."[83] Another tweet from the U.S. Mission to NATO highlights the group's ideational commitments, "SecDef Mattis: For nearly 70 years the #NATO alliance has served to uphold the values upon which our democracies are founded."[84] Similarly, U.S. Ambassador to the United Nations, Linda Thomas-Greenfield, tweeted, "NATO is the most powerful and successful alliance in history, and it's built on the foundation of shared democratic values." Beyond these social dynamics, NATO's attempt to foster a collective identity can also be understood in strategic terms: if its members share an identity, they are more likely to contribute to the organization's overarching goals.[85]

Whatever the motivation, these acts of socialization lead individuals in the community to identify with the larger group. Indeed, American public opinion reflects NATO's dual role as a military alliance and emblem of the democratic community. Survey results summarized in Figure 3 show that most Americans associate "NATO" with the terms *friends*, *democracy*, or *military*. Notably, they are more likely to associate NATO with ideas relevant to a liberal community, such as *friends* and *democracy*, than they are with the Security Council. Another telling result is that *friends* is the most frequently selected term, aligning with the concept of ingroup identification and reflecting NATO's role as more than just a defense alliance.

The third and final part of the argument explains how the liberal democratic community sends social cues regarding humanitarian intervention to ingroup members. Here, countries within the liberal community – especially those institutionalized through NATO – act as cue senders, while citizens in these countries, from laypersons to policymakers and elites, are the recipients. In this setting, social cues take the form of policy positions adopted by foreign governments and institutions like NATO.

Social cues are observed in legislation, legislative votes, and statements or speeches by state officials and leaders, among other behaviors. More broadly, governments and international institutions convey their perspectives through political communication and news media, influencing public discourse. For instance, NATO sent a social cue when the North Atlantic Council voted to

[83] Source (accessed November 10, 2024): twitter.com/nato/status/880498081707565056.

[84] Source (accessed November 10, 2024): https://twitter.com/USNATO/status/1005060527704375296.

[85] See Akerlof and Kranton (2005) for an application of this argument to how economic organizations might benefit from promoting identities among their members. Finnemore (1993) makes a similar argument: States seeking to belong in the community of modernized states will absorb and be taught the norms of IOs.

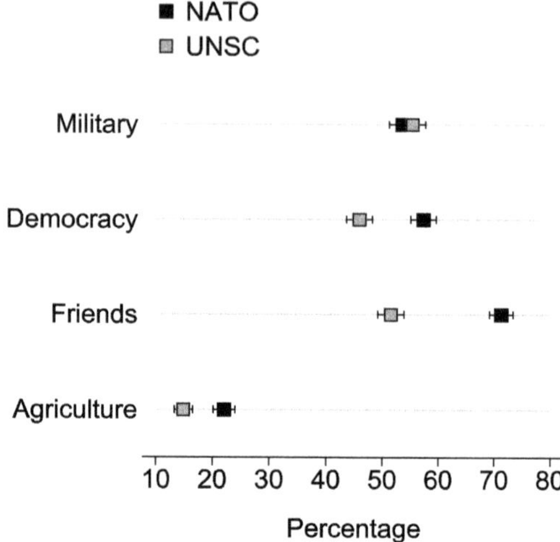

Figure 3 Americans associate "NATO" with the military, democracy, and friends. Question asked, "What do you associate with the [North Atlantic Treaty Organization (NATO)/United Nations Security Council]?" Response options were randomized. *N* = 1,790. Data are from Survey USA-6.

authorize intervention in Kosovo in 1999, a decision relayed through news media and political speeches, such as President Bill Clinton's address to the American public. By contrast, an example of a social cue sent through legislative voting includes the UK Parliament's 2013 vote against a U.S.-led intervention in Syria, which was covered in American news media.[86] Even outside institutional frameworks, individual foreign leaders and other elites can also directly influence public opinion, as Hayes and Guardino (2013) document in their study of the 2003 Iraq War. These policy positions can then be channeled to citizens through the media and the rhetoric of domestic elites attempting to bolster policy support by referencing the endorsements of "foreign voices."

The liberal community's policy endorsements act as social cues that influence members of its ingroup. These social cues exert social pressure, prompting group members to adopt the sender's stance on humanitarian intervention. As theorized, social pressure directly prompts an instinctual alignment with a particular set of preferences or behaviors. They also indirectly mitigate social-relational concerns about the implications of intervention for members of the liberal community. In doing so, social cues address three key questions about how intervening would affect one's country. Is intervention in line with group norms, which include championing liberal values and human rights, and is it

[86] Section 3 discusses these cases in greater detail.

simply appropriate or the right thing to do? Will other ingroup countries also participate in the intervention? Will engaging in intervention harm or improve their country's status or image?[87] The answer to these questions influences people's understanding of pro-norm behavior, group belonging, and status and image, ultimately influencing their support for humanitarian intervention policy.

Next, we can elaborate on the specific role of NATO in institutionalized social cues by the liberal community. As discussed in the general theory, NATO can *clarify* the social meaning of cues sent by its member states while also *amplifying* the reach of these policy endorsements. First, in clarifying social meaning, NATO can help audiences interpret the motives behind a member state's actions. When a state endorses a course of action, it may not be immediately clear whether the support reflects the broader liberal democratic values or narrower national interests. For instance, if the UK backs military intervention, it could be for specific national interests rather than a stance on behalf of the democratic community. However, when the UK makes the same recommendation under NATO's banner, the endorsement takes on a more communal significance, as NATO symbolizes the collective liberal democratic community. In this way, NATO strengthens the social cue by clarifying its social meaning within the democratic community.

Second, NATO serves an amplification role, enhancing the logistical coordination and communication reach among member states and the public. For governments, NATO helps coordinate decisions across the community,[88] increasing the likelihood of reaching shared policy positions, such as on intervention issues. Without this organizational framework, individual governments may struggle to reach or communicate collective decisions. For the public, NATO can increase the prominence of the democratic community's policy cue, as its media presence often surpasses that of any single member state.[89] The following empirical sections highlight how NATO receives substantial coverage in both print and television media, far outpacing individual member states. This visibility supports NATO's role in amplifying the community's voice, ensuring that its policy endorsements reach a broad audience.

In conclusion, social cue theory offers a coherent and distinct perspective on the social dynamics within the liberal community regarding humanitarian

[87] Masumura and Tago (2023) show that multilateral use of force increases a person's evaluation of their country's status.

[88] Keohane 1984; Abbott and Snidal 1998.

[89] E.g., see Chapman 2011, 46 for the salience of the Security Council in U.S. newspapers. The subsequent sections present data from U.S. television news and Japanese newspapers to reinforce this point.

interventions. It suggests that the liberal community can influence democratic citizens through ingroup social cues, which gain even greater power when channeled through institutions like NATO. Furthermore, once citizens receive such a policy endorsement (or rejection) from NATO, they are more likely to discount the views of outgroup members or institutions with mixed identities, such as the Security Council. These cues are influential because they exert social pressure and provide social guidance, helping individuals understand how to fit in and gain good standing within the community of democracies.

2.3 Caveats and Clarifications

This section discusses alternative explanations for NATO's apparent legitimizing effect, the generalizability of the theory, and how the social cue theory contrasts with existing informational theories of international institutions.

2.3.1 NATO's Alternative Effects

The social cue theory predicts that NATO and the liberal community should strongly influence how members of the liberal democracy ingroup think for social identity reasons. But could there be other reasons why these ingroup cues affect people's policy preferences? I lay out two such alternative reasons here, which I evaluate empirically in subsequent sections.

The first alternative explanation relates to people's *material considerations*. People may believe that IOs facilitate burden sharing. If they do, an endorsement by an IO like NATO could imply that their country would have to expend fewer resources to participate in the intervention. While existing research on burden sharing does not necessarily conclude that NATO would be superior to the Security Council in facilitating burden sharing, this is a reasonable alternative explanation.[90] In particular, when NATO supports intervention, it usually means it will commit material resources to that cause. A related material logic is that people may follow NATO's cues because they perceive it to be a strong, competent military alliance capable of conducting military intervention.[91] This military capability relates to burden sharing, but it could also improve the likelihood of a successful intervention, and people tend to like successful policies.[92] All of these material mechanisms relate to the "output" or performance of an institution, which existing research documents as statistically associated with people's perception of institutional legitimacy.[93] The observable

[90] E.g., Martin 1993; Recchia 2015, 2025.
[91] E.g., Bush and Prather (2018) find that Tunisians are influenced by the Arab League in part because they perceive it as a capable organization.
[92] Gelpi, Fever, and Reifler 2009.
[93] Dellmuth and Tallbert 2015.

implication of this material alternative explanation is that people's estimations about the costs and benefits of war should mediate the relationship between NATO's cues and people's support for intervention.

Second, a nonmaterial alternative explanation focuses on *Western regionalism*. It similarly emphasizes identity and ideational factors rather than material and security concerns. Scholars have long observed that NATO, the North Atlantic community, and even the broader liberal community overlap with a racial or geographic group centered in North America and Western Europe.[94] Related work also argues that the "Anglosphere" constitutes a distinct transnational identity that impacts international relations, including forming military coalitions in interstate uses of force.[95] From this perspective, NATO's influence should be understood as an ingroup signal among white Western countries rather than among democracies more generally. One implication of this argument is that NATO's effect should operate only within Western liberal democracies.

Each of these arguments provides an alternative logic for why people might respond more enthusiastically to a NATO-backed intervention compared to one authorized by the Security Council. While they are not necessarily mutually exclusive with the social cue theory (these mechanisms can be additive, for example), the empirical sections demonstrate that they cannot explain away the social cueing mechanisms articulated in my theory.

2.3.2 Generalizing Across Policy Domain, Time, and Political Actors

The influence of social cues could be contingent on three factors. The first is the issue domain. The theory is being applied to the realm of armed humanitarian intervention. Rathbun (2007) observed that, at least among elites, supporting one's community is a fundamental foreign policy value, and such a disposition strongly predicts support for humanitarian military operations. This observation implies that social considerations might be especially important in policies like humanitarian intervention, where other-regarding motivations are salient. In contrast, social considerations might hold less weight for critical national security matters. For example, a country responding to a foreign invader would care little about seeking institutional approval to defend itself.

The second is the time period. The theory in its general form – that IOs representing an identity can send social cues – is being applied to the case of the post–World War II liberal community and, more narrowly, their conduct of

[94] E.g., Hemmer and Katzenstein 2002. [95] Vucetic 2011.

humanitarian interventions since the Cold War. As a social theory, the specific application must be contingent on the social context. For example, it is hard to imagine that a social group of democracies was salient in earlier centuries. Some may also argue that in the era of U.S. President Donald Trump, democracy may once again retrench from being a salient identity grouping in global politics, especially since elites have leeway to shape popular perceptions of legitimacy.[96] However, whether President Trump's rhetoric has fundamentally shifted American identity in world politics remains an open question. In fact, after Trump assailed NATO during his first presidential campaign, the U.S. Congress reacted by bringing forth a bipartisan resolution to affirm the U.S. commitment to NATO.[97] A PEW study also found that "[w]hile Trump recently called into question the value of U.S. participation in NATO, Americans overwhelmingly view NATO membership as beneficial for the United States … Large majorities in both parties say NATO membership is good for the U.S."[98]

In any case, the theory does not claim that identities last forever. While identities and their resulting discourse and mass-level constraints may be stable in the short and medium run,[99] they can change in the long run.[100] Nevertheless, even if the specific application may change, the social cue theory provides fundamental theoretical lessons about social identity and the legitimizing role of institutions in international politics, which I further discuss in the conclusion.

Finally, social cues may operate differently on different political actors. This Element focuses on domestic and international public opinion, which are intrinsically important political actors for the aforementioned reasons. Section 5 provides some evidence regarding foreign elites, but elites are not the focus of my study. So, one might ask, does the theory apply to elites? For example, lawyers in the State Department may prioritize legal considerations. Military elites may prioritize considerations about burden sharing and operational success. Policymakers may already be directly informed about foreign policy matters and do not require a second opinion from an international institution.

But while different elites may have distinct priorities, they are also people, and recent research cast doubt on the exaggerated distinction between elites and the public.[101] One might even argue that when it comes to foreign policy, elites are even more socialized than the mass public into specific modes of

96 Dellmuth and Tallberg 2023.

97 Source (accessed May 31, 2016): http://foreignpolicy.com/2016/05/18/exclusive-in-rebuke-of-trump-house-resolution-defends-nato/.

98 Source (accessed June 14, 2016): www.people-press.org/2016/05/05/public-uncertain-divided-over-americas-place-in-the-world/.

99 Allan, Vucetic, and Hopf 2018, 849.

100 Kranton 2016.

101 Kertzer 2022.

thinking, given their deeper and more direct exposure to international politics. Indeed, the *Washington Post* analyzed polling by the Chicago Council on Global Affairs and found that "[a] new poll suggests that maybe American voters and D.C. foreign policy elites aren't so different after all."[102] Specifically, the analysis found that

> Despite Trump's harsh words about NATO, a consensus exists among all groups polled that the United States should either maintain or increase its commitment to the organization; fewer than 1 in 10 in any group supported leaving NATO. Meanwhile, though Trump had questioned the wisdom of U.S. support for allies such as Japan, South Korea and Germany, there was widespread support for keeping U.S. military bases in these countries.

Corroborating this logic, some existing studies find that IOs do not just influence mass opinion but elites as well. For example, Schultz (2003) argues that a president seeking to wage war can invoke an IO's authorization to help break gridlock among domestic elites. Likewise, Thompson (2009) argues that IOs, and particularly the Security Council, can convince foreign elites to support war. Furthermore, elites themselves often explicitly express their desire for institutional legitimacy. For example, leading up to the 2011 Libyan intervention, top policymakers, including U.S. Secretary of State Hillary Clinton, considered "international authorization" to be a necessary condition for intervention (Chivvis 2014, 55). Lastly, established research on European supranational identity generally implies that elites may be even more socialized in international norms and identity than the mass public, given their direct participation in international politics, travel, and cross-border exchange.[103]

One might point out another way elites differ: they form their opinions in a group setting; however, existing research casts doubt on whether group opinion formation differs fundamentally from that of individuals.[104] Lastly, even if elites like military officers have different priorities,[105] many are still sensitive to pressure from the masses.[106] So, overall, the social cue argument could contribute to understanding elite behavior as well, both directly as elites are subject to social cues and indirectly as they consider the general public.

---

[102] Source (accessed October 13, 2023): www.washingtonpost.com/news/worldviews/wp/2017/04/20/a-new-poll-suggests-that-maybe-american-voters-and-d-c-foreign-policy-elites-arent-so-different-after-all/.

[103] E.g., Risse 2011; Checkel and Katzenstein 2009.

[104] Kertzer 2022.

[105] For example, Recchia (2015) shows how the Security Council can reassure military elites who have concerns about the risks and operational costs of intervention.

[106] Tomz, Weeks, and Yarhi-Milo 2020; Lin-Greenberg 2021; Chu and Recchia 2022.

2.3.3 Contrast with Information Transmission Arguments

While not logically mutually exclusive, the social cue argument is distinct from existing information transmission theories of international institutions in three main ways.[107]

First, existing theories model the process of information-seeking as a means to an end. People seek an informational heuristic to reduce uncertainty about the objective outcomes of a policy. In this case, citizens or foreign elites seek to make an educated guess about whether humanitarian intervention will produce good outcomes. On the other hand, from the social cue perspective, the cue itself is important, and the policy's objective outcome may even be secondary. The cue itself is an act of socialization that creates social pressure while alleviating concerns about norms, status, and group behavior. From the information as a heuristics perspective, cues solve the problem of not having insider or "encyclopedic" knowledge about a policy. From the social cue theory's perspective, even cue recipients with "encyclopedic" knowledge who can make informed decisions would still be influenced by social cues.

Second and closely relatedly, the information transmission and social cue theories focus on different causal mechanisms. Given its emphasis on policy outcomes and motives, information transmission theories tend to focus on the logic of consequences in material, cost-benefit terms. From this view, people are asking questions such as, will intervention cost my country blood and treasure, and will it succeed in achieving the foreign policy objective? Informational cues, as defined in the literature, answer such questions. In contrast, social cues exert social influence and operate through *relational mechanisms*. One could perhaps still call this "social information" and, therefore, also information, but the contents of the mechanism are different. In addition, the social cue theory further emphasizes the effect of direct social pressure, which is not informational in the sense that it causes the cue recipient to update their beliefs about the world.

Lastly, the social cue theory provides a distinct explanation for why some *sources* of cues matter and others do not. Ingroup cues matter most, especially when sent through an institution that has been accepted by the community to represent the identity of the group. In contrast, the information theories present a range of other factors: for example, cues from those with distant policy preferences (i.e., conservative pivotal voters), cues from diverse, independent, or neutral committees, and cues from an elite coalition. These are clearly different theories, primarily drawn from the game theoretic tradition, that lead to different hypotheses about which sources of cues matter.

[107] E.g., Voeten 2005; Fang 2008; Thompson 2009; Chapman 2011.

One final information perspective, also from the game theoretic tradition, that comes closest to the social cue theory argues that cues from *similarly biased* sources can relay useful information as a heuristic.[108] While this perspective has not been fully theorized in the context of IOs and war, the social cue theory does share some insights with these arguments in its focus on like-minded cue givers. Nevertheless, the social cue theory can still differentiate itself for the first two reasons stated earlier: social cues are the object of concern in and of themselves, operating through social pressure and relational mechanisms, rather than a means to an end for the cue recipient to estimate the material consequences of a policy or other behavior. Beyond these two major differences, the social cue theory further provides a deeper set of explanations and testable implications for how socialization and institutionalization of the cue giver affect these dynamics. By contrast, from the informational heuristics perspective, the cue recipient only needs to know the policy preference of the cue sender to update their beliefs based on the cue. Thus, the social cue theory provides a distinct set of propositions about whose cues matter and why, which the remainder of the Element tests.

2.4 Outline of Empirical Sections and Research Designs

The subsequent empirical sections test various implications of the social cue theory as outlined next. Section 3 assesses the effect of social cues sent by the liberal community and NATO in the U.S. context. It does so by examining historical cases and original experimental data from surveys. Section 4 demonstrates the mechanisms of social cues, distinguishing the social causal pathways from material alternative explanations. Section 5 examines the effect of social cues on foreign audiences, and Section 6 (re)assesses arguments from the extant literature relating to international law and information transmission.

- **Observational evidence from American interventions (Section 3):** Historical polls from 1990 to 2013 show that humanitarian interventions backed by the liberal community and NATO enjoy high support from the American people. The Syria case shows that IO approval is critical for raising public support. Comparing Bosnia and Kosovo shows that NATO, with or without the Security Council, can generate public support.
- **Causal evidence of social cues on domestic audiences (Section 3):** Survey experiments show that cues from NATO and the liberal community cause American support for humanitarian intervention to increase. Once Americans learn about NATO's position, the Security Council has little effect, but not the

[108] E.g., Brady and Sniderman 1985; Calvert 1985; Popkin 1994; Lupia and McCubbins 1998.

reverse. These effects are even stronger among the attentive public than among the mass public, implying that NATO's cues are not primarily serving as *informational heuristics* for the ignorant, as existing theories might imply.

- **Institutionalized cues (Section 3):** Additional experiments show that the liberal community's influence on public opinion is more substantial when institutionalized via NATO. Corroborating these experimental results, during the Libya crisis, NATO also received more cable news television coverage than its component countries, showing that IOs receive more salience than specific countries in the real world.
- **Analysis showing the relevance of ingroup perceptions to NATO's influence (Section 4):** NATO's endorsement effect is greatest among (1) those who express the strongest affinity with NATO's member countries and (2) those who associate NATO with democracy and community. In contrast, NATO's influence on public opinion is not impacted by its association with military power, contrary to the *material considerations* alternative explanation.
- **Analysis of the social cue's *relational mechanisms* (Section 4).** NATO's cues activate people's social concerns about norm-abidance, group participation, and status and image. These factors, in turn, affect people's opinions on intervention. In contrast, *material considerations* relating to financial and human costs and benefits cannot fully explain the cueing effect.
- **Foreign audiences (Section 5):** The relative effects of the liberal community, NATO, and the Security Council, as well as the impact of institutionalized cues, reported in Section 2, are all replicated in Japan. This finding contrasts with the alternative explanation of *Western regionalism*. Next, NATO and the Security Council do not significantly affect Egyptian public opinion, but the Arab League does. This finding is also consistent with the social cue theory.
- **Foreign elites (Section 5):** Substantially more members of the United Kingdom Parliament (MPs) would rather receive NATO's backing for humanitarian intervention than the Security Council's if they could only have one or the other.
- **Reconsidering legal perspectives (Section 6).** This section provides additional observational and experimental evidence showing that the Security Council's lack of influence is not due to people's ignorance of international law.
- **Reconsidering arguments about information transmission (Section 6).** Existing theories predict that a neutral and conservative institution like the Security Council should affect public opinion, while a relatively homogenous and hawkish institution like NATO should have a weaker effect. Yet, the evidence thus far shows nearly the opposite. This section presents additional analysis to show that the Security Council's relatively weak effect is not due

to political ignorance. People largely view the Security Council as relatively neutral and conservative. Individual-level data on people's understanding of the Security Council and NATO further show that people's assumptions about institutional neutrality and conservativeness do not moderate the institution's effect on public opinion.

3 Evidence from American Interventions

My fellow Americans, today our armed forces joined our NATO allies in airstrikes against Serbian forces responsible for the brutality in Kosovo.

— Bill Clinton, U.S. President, 1999 address to the American Public

This section tests the claim that democratic countries seeking to boost domestic support for humanitarian intervention can achieve this by securing the endorsement of international institutions. The analysis focuses on the United States, which plays an outsized role in modern humanitarian interventions as either the primary intervening force or a key contributor of financial, political, and military support. If the social cues theory holds, then the liberal democratic community, mainly through NATO, should significantly influence American support for military action.

Drawing on multiple forms of evidence, the following two sections demonstrate that the liberal community and NATO shape American public opinion. The first section explores American views on intervention from Somalia to Syria, using historical polls, media coverage, and presidential speeches from these cases. The second section presents original experimental data from U.S. opinion surveys to assess the causal impact of IOs on public opinion. Consistent with the social cue theory, NATO exerts a distinct causal effect on American public opinion, beyond that of the Security Council. The experimental analysis further separates the impact of IOs from that of their member states, revealing that NATO allows the liberal community to send institutionalized cues that carry more weight than the signals sent by individual member countries alone.

3.1 The Post–Cold War Historical Record

Since the end of the Cold War, armed humanitarian interventions have primarily been a policy of the liberal democratic community, with the United States leading the majority of these actions. Each of these interventions has been multilateral, conducted under the auspices of an international organization such as the Security Council or NATO. Conversely, intervention efforts have been abandoned when institutional approval proved unattainable. This section reviews historical opinion polls from episodes of U.S. interventions, focusing

Table 1 American support for armed humanitarian intervention, from Somalia to Syria

	Endorse Military Action?			% Supporting Military Action	
Cases	**Security Council**	**NATO**	**Liberal Community**	**By Case**	**Average**
Rwanda 1994	No	N/A	Mostly No	28	31
Syria 2013	No	No	No	33	
Kosovo 1999	No	Yes	Yes	53	53
(Libya 2011)	(No)	(Yes)	(Yes)	(56)	(55)
Somalia 1992	Yes	N/A	Mostly Yes	74	55
Haiti 1994	Yes	N/A	Mixed	34	
Bosnia 1994	Yes	Yes	Yes	57	
Libya 2011	Yes	Yes	Yes	56	

Note: This table summarizes data from historical surveys conducted in the United States during episodes of potential humanitarian intervention. NATO is coded N/A when the case was considered "out of area" at the time. The Rwanda poll was taken before France's Operation Turquoise, which received Security Council approval. The Libya case might be classified under "NATO Only" because the Security Council resolution arguably did not cover the airstrikes that led to a regime change. Polls are from the Cornell Roeper Database.

on the case of Syria and a comparative analysis of Bosnia and Kosovo. Syria highlights the challenges of rallying support for unilateral intervention, while the Balkan cases illustrate how NATO can drive humanitarian action with or without Security Council endorsement.

What do the broad, descriptive patterns tell us about the post–Cold War era of humanitarian intervention? Table 1 summarizes the historical relationship between the Security Council, NATO, the liberal community (independent from NATO), and American public support for humanitarian intervention.[109] It includes cases in which the United States considered humanitarian intervention and opinion polling data were available. Column 1 names the case. Columns 2 through 4 give the policy position of the Security Council, NATO, and the liberal community. NATO's policy position on intervention is generally equivalent to the policy position of the liberal community. But when NATO did not consider the case of intervention (i.e., when NATO is N/A in the table), the

[109] The polls cited in this table specifically ask for people's ex ante support for military intervention for humanitarian reasons. They do not include questions like, "Do you agree with how President Clinton is handling the situation in Somalia?"

country positions of the liberal community are coded using public statements and actions of NATO's member states. Finally, Columns 5 and 6 give the percentage of respondents who supported intervention, both for each case and for the aggregation of cases that fall under the same category of multilateralism. The Online Appendix provides detailed notes for each case, its coding, and survey wording.

The record reveals three broad categories of humanitarian intervention: those with no systematic international support (e.g., Syria), those backed by NATO or the club of democracies but not the broader international community via the Security Council (e.g., Kosovo), and those with widespread international backing (e.g., Bosnia). Public opinion across these categories suggests a clear preference among Americans for interventions with international backing. Only 28–31 percent of the public supported intervention without foreign approval, while a majority supported interventions with some degree of IO approval (about a 22–25 percentage point difference in support). Interestingly, in comparing the second and third categories of interventions, Americans do not appear to differentiate interventions with both Security Council and NATO approval from interventions with only NATO approval.[110] These patterns are consistent with the identity theory's prediction that once a cue from the ingroup is received, the additional cue from other countries contributes minimally to public support.

3.1.1 Syria: Unpopular Unilateralism

The case of Syria illustrates the difficulty of legitimizing and mobilizing mass support for humanitarian intervention without broad international approval, even when other factors would predict high support for intervention. Following the Arab Spring, opposition to Syrian President Bashar al-Assad's regime escalated into a civil war by 2012. The conflict was brutal, and there was clear documentation of mass war crimes and human rights violations by the Assad regime.[111]

Several conditions would predict strong public support for intervention in Syria. First, the scale of human rights abuses and civilian casualties in 2011 and 2012 created a significant humanitarian crisis. Second, the civil war created massive international spillover effects. As early as 2012, hundreds of thousands of refugees had already fled the country, and by 2013, that figure grew into the

[110] Some argue that Libya should be classified as a "NATO Only" intervention because the UN Security Council's resolution arguably did not cover the NATO airstrikes against Qaddafi, but reclassifying the Libya case does not change the overall trends.

[111] See, for example, documentation submitted to the UN Human Rights Council under resolutions A/HRC/S-17/1 and A/HRC/Res/19/22.

millions.[112] Third, one of the most widely respected international norms was violated: the taboo against chemical weapons.[113] In 2013, the Syrian government used nerve gas and other chemical weapons to kill over 1,000 civilians.

Fourth, American credibility was on the line. In 2012, President Barack Obama publicly stated that "[w]e have communicated in no uncertain terms with every player in the region that that's a red line for us and that there would be enormous consequences if we start seeing movement on the chemical weapons front or the use of chemical weapons."[114] This view was broadcast widely among the American and international public. Indeed, when chemical weapons were subsequently used, Obama began earnestly courting domestic and international support for military intervention in Syria. If action were not taken in response to the use of chemical weapons, American credibility would be harmed, and Americans have been shown to care about their leaders following through with their promises, including threats.[115]

Fifth, respected domestic elites advocated for military action, particularly within the Democratic Party. President Obama – a highly popular leader – made a strong case for intervention, supported by prominent figures such as Secretary of State John Kerry.[116] These elite endorsements, in theory, should have boosted domestic support for intervention.[117]

Given the scale of the humanitarian disaster, international spillover effects, violation of international norms, cost of American credibility, and elite cues among the Democrats, one would expect high public support for intervention in Syria, especially among Democrats. However, such expectations did not manifest. Multiple opinion polls conducted in late 2012 revealed that less than 35 percent of Americans supported military action, even if intervention was limited to airstrikes. Furthermore, Democrats were about as equally skeptical of intervention as Republicans.[118]

112 Source (accessed November 17, 2023): www.mercycorps.org/blog/facts-syria-crisis.

113 Price 1997; Blair, Chu, and Schwartz 2023 show that Americans largely oppose chemical weapons, while some falsify their permissive preferences about them, reflecting normative prohibition at the domestic level.

114 Obama 2012a.

115 It was not only pundits who believed that American credibility was at stake. President Obama himself stated at a press conference that "American and Congress's credibility is on the line" (Epstein 2013). For evidence on how the public cares about their country's credibility in terms of audience cost dynamics, see Tomz 2008.

116 See Kerry 2013, and also Peter Baker and Michael R. Gordon, "Kerry Becomes Chief Advocate for U.S. Attack – NYTimes.com," *The New York Times*, August 30, 2013, source (accessed November 13, 2015): www.nytimes.com/2013/08/31/world/middleeast/john-kerry-syria.html?pagewanted=all&_r=0.

117 Zaller 1992; Berinsky 2009.

118 See Pew 2013; United Technologies (accessed via Roeper iPoll) 2013.

Why was intervention so unpopular? A close examination of the timing of events with respect to the polling data further helps to triangulate the importance of (lacking) multilateral authorization. When these opinion polls were conducted, the five factors would have predicted a more receptive public. Still, other key factors were consistent with lukewarm public support – namely, the lack of international backing for intervention. Given the Assad regime's ties with Putin, the Security Council vis-à-vis a Russian veto would have rejected any proposal to authorize the use of force. Knowing this, President Obama sought support from crucial ingroup allies like the UK and France for a multilateral and potentially NATO-led intervention. At a press conference in Stockholm, he stated that the "international community's credibility is on the line."[119] But Obama had no luck. In August 2013, the UK Parliament voted against PM David Cameron's proposal to back the United States.[120] France showed similar reluctance. "For months, polls have shown growing opposition among the French for having their military join U.S.-led strikes against Syria [...] French opinion hardened against military action after the UK Parliament voted against intervention on Aug. 29."[121] If the United States were to intervene, it would be unilaterally, but this approach was highly unpopular.

Of course, this case alone cannot draw a definitive causal link between unilateralism and the lack of mass support for intervention in Syria. There are other factors at play, though, as discussed, many of those factors work *against* concluding that unilateralism leads to low public support. One might further question whether American reticence reflects a lack of domestic elite consensus, particularly after 2012 when the Republican Tea Party gained substantial seats in Congress. Failing to secure international approval, Obama did seek the backing of Congress. He was committed to legitimizing intervention by obtaining institutional approval, despite believing he had the authority to initiate an intervention without that approval.[122] Congress did not support Obama; however, this signal of domestic elite disapproval did not come until later in September, *after* the polls cited here.[123] Therefore, careful process tracing shows that domestic elite consensus was not a decisive factor in this case: the American public did not want intervention before Congress rejected Obama's

[119] Epstein 2013.

[120] Source (accessed March 4, 2016): www.bbc.com/news/uk-politics-23892783.

[121] Source (accessed March 4, 2016): http://world.time.com/2013/09/09/et-tu-paris-frances-hollande-faces-growing-opposition-against-syrian-intervention/.

[122] Obama stated, "I possess the authority to order military strikes." Source (accessed November 11, 2023): www.washingtonpost.com/politics/running-transcript-president-obamas-sept-10-speech-on-syria/2013/09/10/a8826aa6-1a2e-11e3-8685-5021e0c41964_story.html.

[123] Source (accessed October 10, 2023): https://abcnews.go.com/Politics/groups-watch-syria-congress/story?id=20214789.

plan, and they still did not want it after.[124] Ultimately, the United States and Russia brokered a deal to remove chemical weapons from Syria,[125] and Obama backpedaled from his red-line threat and decided against intervention.[126]

3.1.2 Kosovo versus Bosnia: What Does the Security Council Approval Add?

A comparison of American attitudes toward U.S. intervention in Bosnia and Kosovo during the 1990s illustrates how NATO's endorsement alone, even without Security Council approval, can be sufficient to garner public support for intervention. The intervention in Bosnia received both Security Council and NATO backing, while the intervention in Kosovo was supported solely by NATO, authorized through its North Atlantic Council. Despite this difference, American public opinion on the two interventions was remarkably similar: 57 percent supported intervention in Bosnia, and 53 percent supported intervention in Kosovo – a negligible difference, or what might be called a "null effect" in statistical terms. This raises a key question: if the Security Council is essential for legitimizing military action, why did its absence in Kosovo have so little impact on public opinion?

One might speculate that the Security Council's approval did substantially boost public support for intervention in Bosnia, but that other factors counteracted its legitimizing effect. This is possible, yet any plausible counteracting factors between the two cases are either similarly present in each case or differ in ways that should have increased, rather than diminished, support for Bosnia.

To start with the similarities, both interventions took place in the same geographic region, with similar proximity to NATO, and involved conflicts with shared historical and cultural roots. While Bosnia and Kosovo were, of course, distinct conflicts, they likely evoked similar associations among the American public – certainly more so than two conflicts in regions like Southeast Asia and sub-Saharan Africa might have. Additionally, both interventions were initiated under the same U.S. president, Bill Clinton, whose leadership likely shaped public sentiment toward each intervention. Public opinion on foreign policy often reflects the influence of the sitting president, the most visible decision-maker in this realm.

[124] As mentioned, even Democrats largely opposed intervention, so public opposition cannot be purely driven by Tea Party momentum.

[125] Source (accessed October 13, 2023): www.nytimes.com/2013/09/15/world/middleeast/syria-talks.html.

[126] Other factors that may have worked against Obama include the 2008 financial crisis and fatigue from Iraq and Afghanistan. These factors also existed in the Libya case, but the outcome of Libya differed substantially.

What about the differences between Bosnia and Kosovo, besides the degree of institutional backing? There are at least three salient differences, but two of them should have increased public support for intervention in Bosnia over Kosovo, thereby adding rather than subtracting from the Security Council's legitimizing effect. First, there is the issue of timing and potential war weariness, a well-documented factor in American foreign policy. Public tolerance for military intervention tends to wane over time, especially if there is a perception that the United States is overextended or becoming embroiled in too many conflicts. But in this case, Bosnia preceded Kosovo. If war wariness were an overriding factor, then the American public should have reacted to Kosovo with "not another Eastern European intervention." But without the Security Council's blessing, the Kosovo intervention enjoyed almost as high support as Bosnia. Second, there is the nature of the humanitarian crisis. In both cases, tens of thousands of innocents were killed in war crimes, but governments used stronger normative language in Bosnia. In Bosnia, the language of genocide was often invoked, including by the UN General Assembly. When it came to Kosovo, commentators, lawyers, and institutions framed the crisis as ethnic cleansing – a grave term but not as legally or morally charged as "genocide."[127] For example, the *Wall Street Journal* reported, "Despite Tales, the War in Kosovo Was Savage, but Wasn't Genocide."[128] Given that "genocide" holds a greater resonance in humanitarian and human rights discourse, one to expect the public to be more supportive of intervention in Bosnia, the case with Security Council backing, but it did not.

A third factor that does cut against the Security Council's legitimization in Bosnia is the fact that Bosnia involved "boots on the ground," whereas Kosovo was limited to airstrikes. Americans are generally more reticent about sending ground troops,[129] likely due to the increased risk of casualties. So, of these three factors firmly established in the literature – war wariness, humanitarian considerations, and type of intervention – two of them should theoretically have raised support for intervening in Bosnia, in conjunction with the Security Council's approval. Thus, it is difficult to decisively argue that Security Council approval in Bosnia was being consistently reversed by other factors.

In sum, comparing the interventions in Bosnia and Kosovo helps us examine the relationship between the Security Council and public opinion, conditional

[127] Contrast the Wikipedia articles on the "Bosnian Genocide" versus "War Crimes in Kosovo," which includes primary source references to how international institutions like the UN and international courts described the two crises (accessed October 13, 2023).

[128] Source (accessed October 13, 2023): www.wsj.com/public/resources/documents/pearl123199.htm.

[129] Recchia and Chu 2021, 924.

on NATO's support being present. There appears to be little systematic relationship. Instead, President Clinton rallied as much public support for intervening in Kosovo as in Bosnia. It is telling that in his speech justifying war to the American people, he invoked the fact that the United States would be intervening with "NATO" and "allies" almost as frequently as he appealed to humanitarian considerations regarding brutality and the death of the innocent.[130] These cases illustrate that, throughout America's significant history of humanitarian intervention, securing the endorsement of the liberal community and NATO has been crucial.

3.2 Experimental Evidence

The historical record suggests a significant role of institutional legitimacy – particularly the approval of fellow democracies and NATO – in shaping public support for humanitarian intervention. Nonetheless, questions remain about whether international institutions *cause* public opinion to change. First, one may wonder if public opinion itself influenced institutional decisions, rather than institutions shaping public opinion. For instance, in Syria, perhaps France and Germany hesitated to support intervention because they perceived that American public reticence would be challenging to overcome, even with their endorsement. Second, others may point to idiosyncratic factors rather than systematic patterns about NATO and the Security Council as the primary drivers of public opinion. The scarcity of cases could make it particularly difficult to refute this critique. For example, Somalia was the U.S. first major humanitarian intervention following the widely popular Gulf War, and the public's enthusiasm may have been fueled by the "warm glow" of that recent victory, rather than by any international consensus. In the case of Syria, one might argue that religious bias, rather than the lack of institutional backing, reduced public support for intervening on behalf of the primarily Muslim victims of civil war.[131] Both selection bias and case-specific idiosyncrasies could, therefore, interfere with establishing causality.

To address these questions, the following section turns to experimental evidence from original surveys to assess whether NATO's cues directly influence public opinion. In addition, these survey experiments then disentangle the effect of the broader community of democratic countries from their institutionalized cues sent through NATO – something historical data alone cannot achieve.

---

[130] Source (accessed November 12, 2023): https://edition.cnn.com/ALLPOLITICS/stories/1999/03/25/clinton.transcript/#:~:text=PRESIDENT%20CLINTON%3A%20My%20fellow%20Americans,from%20a%20mounting%20military%20offensive.

[131] Chu and Lee 2024.

3.2.1 Research Design of Survey Experiments

My research strategy for isolating the effect of IOs is to embed experiments about humanitarian intervention within public opinion surveys. In this section, I present evidence from three of these surveys conducted in the United States from 2015 to 2017. These surveys included several questions designed to test the social cue theory, and the centerpiece of the survey asked the survey takers to read a hypothetical news article about a violent humanitarian crisis in which "[m]ilitary groups fighting in [foreign country] have killed thousands of civilians, including women and children, and have left tens of thousands homeless and starving." The "[foreign country]" is randomly displayed as Azerbaijan, Burma (Myanmar), Chad, Colombia, or Yemen, which are all countries representing different regions with a history of civil conflict.

Next, in the news article, respondents read about the Security Council and NATO's stance on using military force, and this is where the experiment comes in. In the first survey, respondents were randomly assigned to read one of three potential scenarios: both NATO and the Security Council oppose intervention (*Both Oppose*), only NATO supports intervention (*NATO Only*), and both IOs endorse intervention (*Both Endorse*). The U.S. government supports intervention across all of the treatment groups, so only the endorsement of international institutions is randomized. After all, it's a moot point if the U.S. government does not want to intervene.

The second and third surveys include an additional or slightly modified set of scenarios designed to evaluate what happens when only the Security Council endorses intervention (*UNSC Only*) and the potential distinct effects of the liberal community versus its cue via NATO. I will elaborate upon these two surveys later in the section.

Finally, after reading about the humanitarian crisis and the policy stances of the two IOs, the survey respondents are asked to express their support for armed humanitarian intervention. "In this situation, do you support or oppose the US sending its military to help civilians in [country]?" There were six possible replies: support or oppose a little, a moderate amount, or a great deal, but the following analysis reports the binary outcome support versus oppose intervention, for ease of interpretation. Respondents' answers to this question form the study's primary dependent variable: *Support for Intervention*. The full text of these surveys appears in the Online Appendix.

3.2.2 NATO and the Security Council's Cueing Effect

The first survey, administered to a nationally representative sample of Americans by YouGov, allows us to estimate the main effect of IOs on public opinion (Survey

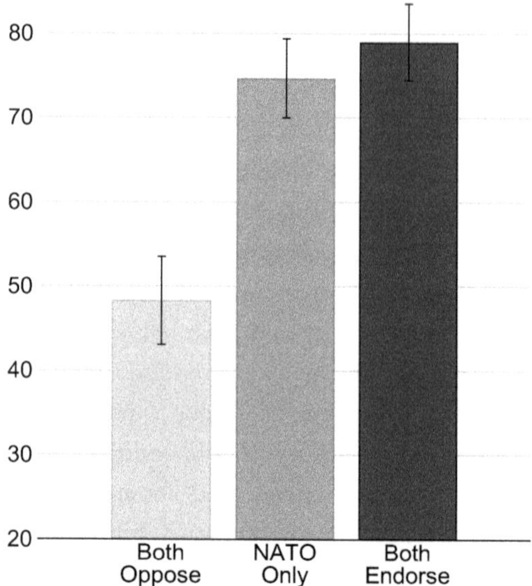

Figure 4 NATO raises support for intervention, the Security Council adds a little extra. This figure shows the percentage of respondents supporting intervention depending on NATO and the Security Council's stance on intervention. 95% confidence intervals are given. $N = 1{,}000$. Data are from Survey USA-1.

USA-1). Figure 4 summarizes its results and shows that moving from a situation where NATO and the Security Council oppose intervention (*Both Oppose*) to one where NATO endorses intervention but not the Security Council (*NATO Only*) raises *Support* by 26.4 percentage points (pp.). This difference is a substantial and statistically significant effect ($p<0.01$). By contrast, the additional impact of the Security Council's endorsement (moving from *NATO Only* to *Both Endorse*) is substantively small (4.3 pp.) and statistically insignificant ($p = 0.20$). Thus, as hypothesized, an ingroup cue from NATO raises public support for war, and once the ingroup cue is received, the broader cue from the Security Council has little effect.

Bolstering the external validity of these findings, the 26.4 pp. effect derived from the experiment mirrors the historical polling data shown in the previous section, which estimated a 22 pp. difference between the *NATO only* and dual endorsement scenarios. Furthermore, these effects are robust to (if not even larger) examining only the informed public or liberal internationalists, implying that the effect is present among those informed about international affairs.[132]

[132] This analysis is in the Online Appendix. Wittkopf (1990, Ch. 5) finds that elites are more internationalist than the public. Milner and Tingley (2016) find that liberal internationalists are a key coalition in U.S. foreign policy.

NATO's more substantial impact on the informed public also implies that its cues are not exclusively operating as a heuristic to solve the problem of rational ignorance, as some informational theories would predict.

I now turn to Survey USA-2, which replicates the three scenarios in the first survey but adds a fourth scenario in which only the Security Council but not NATO supports intervention (*UNSC Only*). This scenario is unusual from a historical standpoint since there is no case in which NATO rejects intervention but the Security Council, which includes veto-holding NATO members, endorses intervention. Nevertheless, this hypothetical situation can be used to evaluate the social cue theory. Specifically, critics may argue that the results displayed in Figure 3 should be interpreted as a generic first versus second cue effect. The fact that receiving *NATO Only* has a large effect and *IOs Endorse* does not further boost public opinion is an artifact of NATO providing the first cue, while any second cue will be less valuable. While plausible, the data do not support this critique.

The left-hand side of Figure 5 shows the level of public support in each of the four conditions from Survey USA-2. It replicates the main results from Survey #1, where *NATO Only* was substantially higher than *Both Oppose*, but *Both Endorse* is trivially greater than *NATO Only*. In contrast, while *UNSC Only* increases public support, the additional endorsement of NATO in *Both Endorse* still generates additional (and even more) public support. The right-hand side of the figure combines NATO and the Security Council's effect sizes conditional

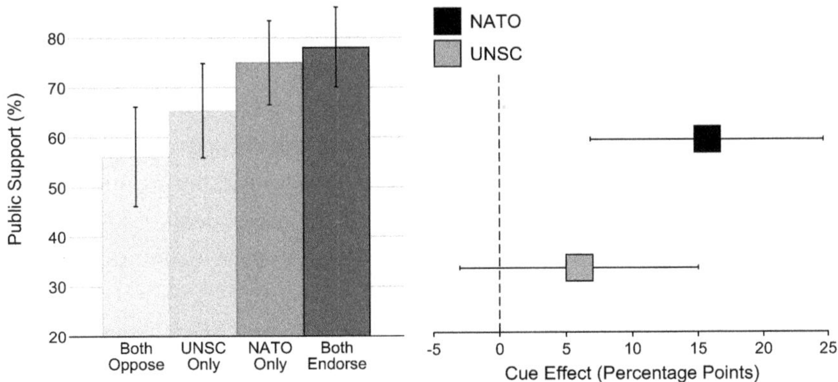

Figure 5 NATO has a greater effect than the Security Council. The figure on the left shows public support for intervention in four scenarios regarding NATO and the Security Council's stance on intervention. The figure on the right reports the average treatment effect of each IO. 95% confidence intervals are given. $N = 408$. Data are from Survey USA-2.

on each other into an average effect. It shows that the effect of NATO is 15.7 pp., and the Security Council is 6 pp. These results demonstrate that NATO exerts greater influence on American public opinion than the Security Council, not just when it is the first policy endorser. Furthermore, these data refute the view that citizens cannot distinguish between NATO and the Security Council. Finally, these results cannot be easily explained by legal and informational theories, which hypothesize that an affirmative endorsement by the Security Council should raise public support for a policy. The results are instead consistent with the social cue perspective on the centrality of ingroup cues.

3.2.3 The Power of Institutionalized Cues

In the first two surveys, survey takers read information about the IOs and their member countries in conjunction. This research design choice increases the realism of the survey: news and political speeches relating to IOs and military intervention generally mention both the IO and key countries.[133] However, such a design cannot disentangle the effect of the IOs from their component countries, which is required to evaluate the social cue theory's argument about the power of institutionalized cues. To answer these questions, this section thus turns to additional experimental and observational analysis.

Beginning with the experimental data, a third survey seeks to disaggregate the effect of NATO's cue from the effect of its member countries sending a cue without NATO (Survey USA-3). The survey experimentally split the respondents into three groups, each with two sub-conditions (3x2). As in the previous surveys, the first one-third of the respondents were experimentally assigned to read that "The North Atlantic Treaty Organization (NATO) [supports/opposes] taking military action to help these civilians. NATO members include the U.S., Canada, and several European countries." Then, to distinguish the effect of NATO from the effect of its named countries, the second one-third of the respondents read about the policy position of NATO without mention of any particular country, while the final one-third of the respondents read about the policy position of "U.S., Canada, and several European countries" without mention of NATO.

Thus, this design creates six experimental groups: *Only Countries*, *Only NATO*, or *Both Countries and NATO* either support or oppose military action.[134] As before, the dependent variable measures public support for

[133] For example, when the Security Council authorizes the use of force, news articles will often also mention the voting record of the permanent five members.

[134] Because Surveys #1 and #2 already show that NATO's effect is independent of the Security Council, this version did not mention and vary the Security Council's policy position, which helps to increase the NATO experiment's statistical power.

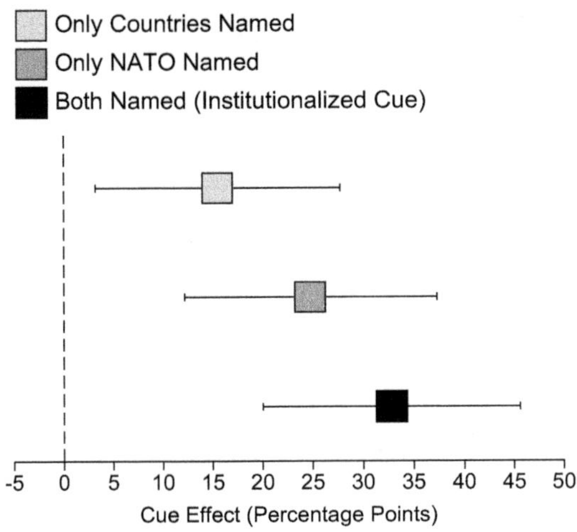

Figure 6 The liberal community's cue has a stronger effect when it is sent through NATO. This figure shows the cue effect on public support for intervention in percentage points, depending on whether countries in the liberal community, NATO, or both are explicitly named in the experiment. $N = 598$. Data are from Survey USA-3.

intervention. Figure 6 summarizes the results of this survey. When the liberal community sends a social cue (*Only Countries Named Support – Oppose*), public support for war shifts by about 15.5 pp. When it sends the same cue via NATO (*Both Named*), public support shifts by about 32.8 pp. The effect of naming *only NATO* is included to be comprehensive but is challenging to interpret. Even though it does not mention NATO's member countries, respondents can easily infer that several democratic countries support intervention simply from hearing "NATO." What this data does help to clarify, though, is whether the cue's effect relies primarily on naming countries. The results show they do not: the cue effect under that condition is 24.8 pp., which is less than 32.8.

Lastly, the social cue theory states that institutions do not just clarify the social meaning of a cue, but they can also play a logistical and communication role by increasing the cue's reach. Without NATO, individual governments in the liberal community might not otherwise be able to coordinate on a policy position and subsequently ensure that their policy viewpoints reach the ears of various domestic audiences. This point cannot be tested in a survey experiment, since all survey takers are shown the social cue directly. Furthermore, it is difficult to establish the causal effect of institutionalization on a cue's accessibility and reach in the real world, as it is impossible to randomize the existence of NATO. Nevertheless, observational data can help to assess the claim's

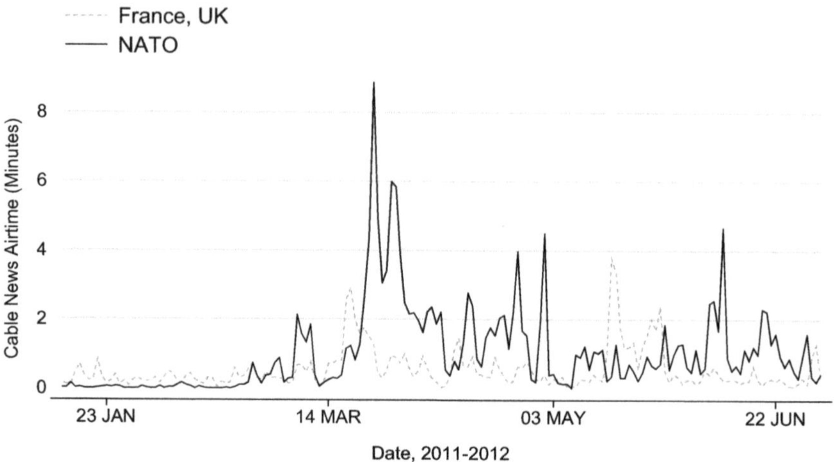

Figure 7 NATO receives more cable news airtime than its member countries. This figure measures the TV news salience of NATO versus specific NATO countries surrounding the Libyan intervention episode. The graph is produced by the Stanford Cable TV News Analyzer, available at (accessed on 10 November 2024): https://tvnews.stanford.edu/. The web tool is for "count[ing] the screen time of who and what is in cable TV news . . . The dataset includes near 24-7 recordings of CNN, Fox News, and MSNBC."

plausibility. Figure 7 summarizes data from American cable television collected by the Stanford Cable TV News Analyzer. The data capture the number of minutes per day certain topics are discussed on CNN, MSNBC, and Fox News. According to this data, during the 2011 Libyan intervention episode, NATO generally received more airtime on American cable TV than the individual NATO countries advocating for intervention, France, and the United Kingdom. This pattern is consistent with the theory's claim that institutionalized cues receive more exposure among the general public.

Taken together, the historical and experimental evidence in this section demonstrate that the liberal community and NATO have a powerful effect on American attitudes toward humanitarian intervention, one that is potentially even stronger than the Security Council. Furthermore, cues by the liberal community have more impact and greater reach when channeled through NATO.

4 Evidence of Social Cueing

The evidence thus far supports the social cue theory by showing that NATO and the liberal community affect mass support for humanitarian intervention. This section now directly assesses the causal mechanisms that explain *why* NATO affects public opinion, drawing from the data on the American public. The identity theory argues that, because Americans identify with NATO's member countries, NATO raises support for intervention by revealing the social implications of deploying military force. NATO can also shift public opinion directly by exerting social influence. This argument contrasts with an alternative explanation that views NATO's effect as primarily relaying information about military capabilities and material burden sharing.

This section tests three implications of the social cue theory's causal processes. First, the NATO effect should be the largest among Americans who most closely identify with NATO's member countries and who view NATO as an ingroup institution, and not necessarily those who view NATO in terms of its military strength. Second, causal mediation analysis should reveal that NATO affects public opinion via the three *relational mechanisms*: norm abidance, group participation, and status and image. Third, the effect of NATO should not be entirely eliminated after ruling out people's material cost and benefit calculations.

4.1 Test #1: Examine Subgroups That View NATO as an Ingroup

The social cue theory implies that NATO's effect is most substantial among Americans who identify with its member countries and view NATO as an ingroup community of fellow democracies. I test this hypothesis in two ways. First, I examine how NATO's effect on public support for military intervention varies depending on individuals' affinity with NATO member countries. To do so, in Survey USA-2, respondents were asked whether they perceive Canada, Germany, France, and the United Kingdom as having a "friendly," "neutral," or "hostile" relationship with the United States.[135] For the analysis, I then divided the sample into two groups based on respondents' average affinity with these four countries.

Figure 8 shows that NATO's cueing effect is about 6.9 percentage points (pp.) among those with relatively low affinity for the four NATO countries, whereas it reaches 22.6 pp. among those with high affinity for these countries. The difference in effect sizes is substantially large, about 16 pp. ($p = 0.086$). These findings support the theory: NATO's cues have a notably stronger impact on Americans who feel a closer connection to its member countries.

Turning to a second approach, I estimated the effect of NATO's cue on different groups of people, depending on how they understood NATO (Survey

[135] The survey also asked about China and Russia. Together, this encompasses two countries that are only in NATO, only in the Security Council, and in both IOs. Data on all countries are in the Online Appendix.

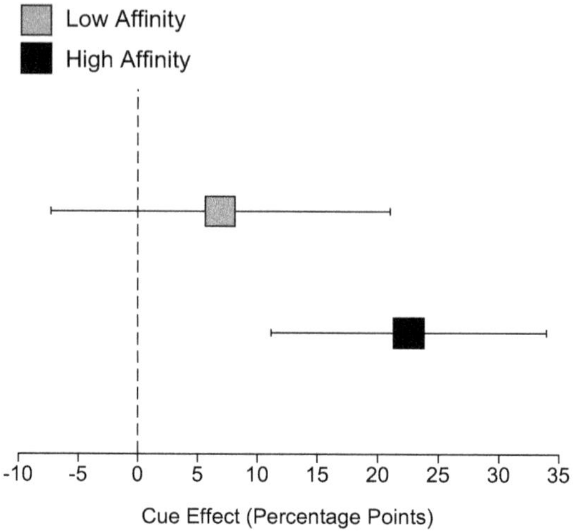

Figure 8 NATO's effect is greater among Americans expressing high affinity with NATO's members. This figure reports the effect of NATO's endorsement on public support for intervention among survey takers with Low or High Affinity with NATO's member countries. 95% confidence intervals are given. $N = 408$. Data are from Survey USA-2.

USA-3). To measure people's understanding of NATO, the survey asked, "When you hear 'NATO,' which of the following words or phrases come to mind? Please select all apply." The survey taker could then choose from a list of choices that include *friends* and *democracy*, which were relevant to the liberal community concept, in addition to *military*, *agriculture*, *foreign investment*, *freeloaders*, *enemies*, *none/don't know*. The order of these choices was randomly displayed. About 80 percent of the respondents selected *friends*, *democracy*, or *military*, consistent with the "correct" understanding of NATO.[136]

With this data, I classified individuals who selected "friends" or "democracy" as explicitly perceiving NATO as a liberal community. I then estimated NATO's cue effect among this group. The social cue theory predicts that NATO will have a more substantial impact on this group than those outside of it. To examine the *material considerations* alternative explanation, I also classified individuals who selected "military" as seeing NATO from a security perspective and then similarly estimated NATO's impact on members of this group compared to those outside of it. Figure 9 displays the results of this analysis.

[136] 3 percent Agriculture; 6 percent Enemies; 7 percent Freeloaders; 6 percent Don't Know; 34 percent Foreign Investment. In retrospect, the jargon "foreign investment" could have been interpreted as "investing in foreign stuff," which might have led to the unusual high response in this category. Overall, however, this data shows that the mere acronym "NATO" was interpreted by a substantial amount of the sample in an intelligible way.

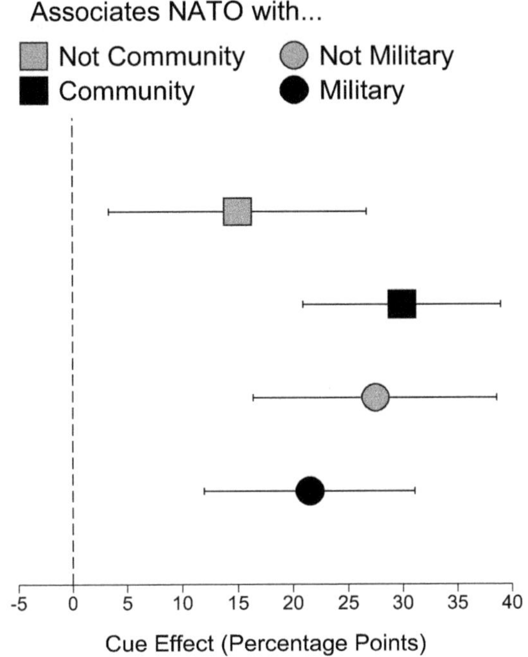

Figure 9 NATO's effect is stronger among Americans who associate it with community, not military. This figure reports the effect of NATO's endorsement on public support for war depending on whether or not respondents associated NATO with "democracy" or "friend" (i.e., community) or "military." 95% confidence intervals are given. $N = 598$. Data are from Survey USA-3.

Consistent with the social cue theory, NATO's effect is about 15 pp. among those who did not associate NATO with the words *friend* or *democracy*, while it is nearly double, about 30 pp., among those who do. Thus, NATO's impact on public opinion operates not only via general affinity, as the previous analysis in Figure 8 showed, but specifically via ingroup belonging over the substantive issue of *democracy*.

By contrast, whether people associate NATO with the military or not, NATO's cueing effect is about the same. If anything, associating NATO with the military reduces NATO's influence. This dampening effect is about −6 pp., though it is statistically indistinguishable from zero ($p = 0.42$). These patterns show that NATO's cueing effect cannot be explained by Americans liking the idea of a strong military organization backing their foreign policy. On the contrary, Americans may possibly be sensitive to the prospects of their country warmongering abroad, so NATO's military reputation can be detrimental to its influence on domestic legitimacy. While the social cue theory needed not to be incompatible with the alternative explanation of military capabilities, as both logics could operate simultaneously, these findings ultimately only confirmed the social perspective.

4.2 Test #2: Directly Estimate Social Causal Mechanisms

This second test analyzes six causal mechanisms (or mediators) that might explain NATO's effect on public support for war.[137] The first three relational mechanisms are associated with the social cue argument. The mechanism *Norm Abidance* captures beliefs about whether intervention conforms to liberal humanitarian norms about using military force for humanitarian reasons.[138] *Group Participation* indicates respondents' beliefs about whether other countries will join the operation. *Benefit Status/Image* measures perceptions about whether an intervention would improve or damage the U.S. "reputation."[139] The next three mechanisms are unrelated to the social cue theory, though the social cue theory does not rule them out either. The mechanism *Prevent Contagion* indicates people's expectations about whether *not* intervening would lead to a spread of conflict. *Retaliation Unlikely* records beliefs about whether other countries would punish the United States for using military force. *Casualties Unlikely* measures expectations about American casualties.

To what extent does each of these six causal mechanisms serve as a link between NATO's cue and public opinion? Answering these questions involves using a statistical procedure called causal mediation analysis,[140] which has three steps. The first step estimates the effect of the treatment (i.e., NATO) on each mediator. The second step estimates the effect of each mediator on the outcome, support for war. The third and final step uses statistical information from the first two steps in a simulation process to estimate how much the treatment's effect on the outcome is channeled through each mediator.

Figure 10 displays the results from steps one and two. The left panel shows the effect of NATO's cue on each mediator. The estimated probit coefficients are

137 Returning to data from Survey USA-1.

138 Considerations about what is pro-norm could, however, take a less concrete form and reflect beliefs that intervention is simply the right thing to do or morally appropriate. Thus, this survey measure cannot capture the broader concept and might be interpreted as an underestimate of the social cue theory's mechanism.

139 The survey asked respondents to evaluate how intervention would affect the U.S. "reputation," generically speaking (i.e., not a reputation for resolve or something else specifically). Reputation is a more colloquial term that captures the academic concepts of status and image, which are jargon. However, the colloquial use of reputation is probably closer to image but not the hierarchical concept of status.

140 Imai et al. 2011.

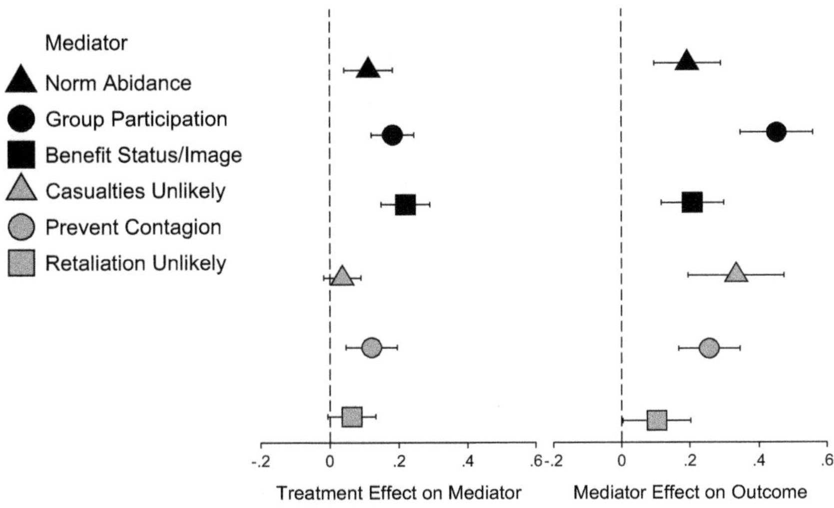

Figure 10 Potential mediators that explain NATO's effect. This figure gives the predicted marginal effects from probit coefficient estimates. The left panel plots the NATO effect on six mediators, and the right panel plots those mediators' effect on people's intervention support, controlling for potential confounds. The treatment, mediator, and outcome variables are binary. Estimates from the control variables are not displayed. Each of the 12 estimates is obtained from a separate regression (N=685). 95% confidence intervals are given. Data are from Survey USA-1.

reported in terms of predicted probabilities. When NATO recommends intervention, people are more likely to believe that intervention benefits U.S. status, will attract group participation, and will follow liberal humanitarian norms. Additionally, NATO's policy cues make people more likely to believe that intervention can prevent crisis contagion, while it does not significantly change people's beliefs about the chances of international retaliation and casualties. The right panel illustrates each mediator's effect on people's support for intervention. The mediators are not experimentally varied, so I include control variables to reduce confounding from omitted variables.[141] Each mediator affects people's support for humanitarian intervention but to different degrees. Concerns about status have the most considerable effect, while fears of retaliation have the smallest effect.

[141] The control variables are gender, age, education, income, race, religion, ideology, political party, voter registration, internationalism, human rights beliefs, and news interest. Their estimates are in the Online Appendix.

Table 2 Social-relational factors mediate NATO's effect on public opinion

Mediator	**Mediation Effect (Percentage Points)**
Norm Abidance	**1.5**
Group Participation	**3.9**
Benefit Status/Image	**6.7**
Casualties Unlikely	1.3
Prevent Contagion	**3.2**
Retaliation Unlikely	0.6
Remaining NATO Effect Unexplained	9.2

Note: This table shows the mediation effects of six factors that might explain why NATO raises support for intervention. Bolded numbers indicate statistical significance at the 0.05 level. N=527. Data are from Survey USA-1.

Combining these two steps allows me to estimate each mediator's average causal mediation effect (ACME),[142] or the extent to which each mediator can explain why NATO's cues influence public opinion on war. Table 2 reports each ACME. Recall Section 3 in which Survey USA-1 revealed that NATO raises public support by about 26.4 pp. Beginning at the top of the table, the analysis shows that 1.5 of those 26.4 pp. are channeled through people's changing beliefs about whether intervention would be consistent with humanitarian objectives and thus pro-norm.[143] The results show that the other two social mechanisms – group participation and status/image considerations – are also substantial and statistically significant. NATO's effect on public opinion also owes to its ability to shift beliefs about whether the humanitarian crisis would spread (*Prevent Contagion*), which is not predicted by the social cue theory, nor is it contradictory to the theory.

Meanwhile, people's expectations about international punishment and casualties are not significant mediators.[144] The last row reports the amount of

[142] The analysis executes the procedures outlined in Imai et al. (2011) using statistical software programmed by Hicks and Tingley (2011). The Online Appendix gives a technical overview of this analysis.

[143] As mentioned earlier, this is probably an underestimate of the norm abidance mechanism since it only measures humanitarian norms and not broader impressions of appropriateness.

[144] The statistically insignificant "casualty effect" might seem unusual. But to clarify, it does not contradict the claim that casualties affect public opinion (e.g., Mueller 1973; Gartner 2008). The

NATO's effect left unexplained by the mediation analysis: its overall 26.4 pp. effect minus the sum of all six mediation effects. Recall that the social cue theory argues that NATO exerts direct social pressure on ingroup members: presumably, some of this direct pressure is captured by the 9.2 pp. left unexplained by the causal mediation model, but this interpretation cannot be tested explicitly. In any case, the mediation analysis directly supports the social cue theory's interpretation of legitimacy as alleviating relational concerns.

4.3 Test #3: Ruling Out Non-Social Mechanisms

This final test shows that NATO's endorsement effect remains *even after* explicitly accounting for "objective" cost-benefit factors, such as the number of lives that would be saved, the financial and human costs of military action, and the mode of intervention. To rule out these alternative factors, Survey USA-4 included the original experiment in which NATO supports or opposes military action (*NATO*), while additionally randomizing whether respondents received or did not receive information about military action's material cost and benefits. Specifically, those who received information read that "[m]ilitary action would save the lives of about [80 thousand OR 620 thousand] civilians. The operation would cost the U.S. government about [$850 million OR $4.1 billion], but the U.S. would avoid risking casualties by not sending ground troops." Those who did not receive the information received no additional text.

If NATO's cue raises public support for intervention by providing information about the *material consequences* of military action, directly providing that information to respondents should reduce the effect of NATO. However, the analysis is summarized in Figure 11 and shows that informing people about the material costs of intervention does not substantially reduce the effect of NATO's cues. When the information treatment holds constant the financial and human cost of intervention, NATO shifts public opinion by 26.9 pp. When these factors are not fixed, the effect of NATO drops slightly but insubstantially to 25.7 pp.[145] Thus, these material burden-sharing factors cannot fully explain NATO's effect on public opinion.[146]

right panel of Figure 9 shows that *Casualties* affect *Support*, but it is just that IO approval does not affect *Casualties*.

145 The Online Appendix shows NATO's effect under different degrees of financial cost and estimated lives saved. People generally prefer more beneficial interventions at lower costs, but the substantive conclusions about NATO are orthogonal and remain the same.

146 This resonates with existing research. In a study of how the EU signals to investors, Gray (2009) discovers that once "the EU endorses a country's policies, market expectations for that country's performance converge. Interestingly, this suggests that markets pay less attention to the actual path of reform than to the EU pronouncements on it" (Gray 2009, 932).

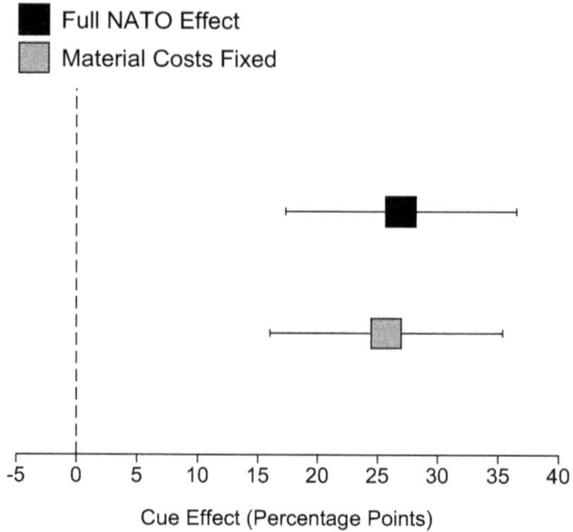

Figure 11 Material factors (financial costs and anticipated casualties) do not explain NATO's effect. This figure reports the effect of NATO on public support for intervention depending on whether survey takers received information about the material costs of intervention (i.e., whether the material costs are "fixed"). $N = 766$. Data are from Survey USA-4.

5 Foreign Audiences

Sections 3 and 4 demonstrate how social cues from the liberal community and NATO affect domestic (in this case, American) public opinion on armed humanitarian intervention. This section turns to international opinion, focusing on public and elite audiences within liberal democratic countries. There are three reasons for this focus, the first two having to do with practical relevance and the last with theory. First, liberal democracies are the primary countries directly participating in multilateral humanitarian interventions. Second, public opinion is more likely to affect international politics in democratic than in autocratic countries.[147] Lastly, the social cue theory is about how institutionalized cues help to rally ingroup members, which in this case is the community of democracies.

For these reasons, the evidence next examines the Japanese public and members of parliament (MPs) in the United Kingdom as cases of foreign audiences relevant to American intervention policy. That said, this section also assesses how IOs affect public opinion in Egypt, a country outside the liberal community. The theory does not rule out NATO affecting Egyptian

[147] Public opinion can affect the foreign policy of autocratic governments but likely less consistently and directly than in the democratic context (Weeks 2008, 2014).

public opinion because some Egyptians might respond to NATO for reasons not theorized here. Still, the theory does imply that institutions with more proximate identities, such as the Arab League, should exert more substantial influence.

To preview, these analyses produce three main results. First, social cues by the liberal community, especially when institutionalized by NATO, affect Japanese public opinion. These results from Japan are particularly useful for pushing back against alternative explanations that cast NATO as only impacting the Western world or Anglosphere. Second, MPs in the UK Parliament preferred an intervention backed by NATO over the Security Council when forced to choose only one of the two. Lastly, in Egypt, a side-by-side experimental comparison of cues from the Security Council, NATO, and the Arab League reveals that only the Arab League significantly affects public opinion. These findings support the social cue theory.

5.1 Japanese Public Opinion on U.S. Intervention

This section shows how cues from the liberal community and NATO influence Japanese support for U.S. intervention. But before doing so, I elaborate on the political and theoretical relevance of the Japan case.

5.1.1 Why Japan?

Evaluating the social cue theory in Japan produces both practical and theoretical insights. First of all, Japan is a critical player in U.S. foreign policy and collaborates directly with NATO, making U.S. soft power in Japan politically important. Japan's postwar constitution limits its ability to use military force, and it thus relies on the United States for security. Nevertheless, Japan retains substantial foreign policy discretion, such as in its foreign aid programs and deployment of noncombat troops (i.e., its Self Defense Force or SDF). During the post-WWII period, Japan joined the United Nations and has become particularly active in activities like peacekeeping.

Furthermore, since the early 1990s, especially with Japan's growing wariness of China and disillusionment with the Security Council,[148] Japan deepened its association with NATO. Japan is one of NATO's "partners across the globe" and cooperates with NATO across several domains, such as humanitarian relief and state building. For example, Japan contributed over $2 billion to the NATO-led International Security Assistance Force in Afghanistan.[149] The highest levels of

[148] Japan has been unsuccessful in joining the Security Council's permanent membership (Reinhard 2000).

[149] Source (accessed April 11, 2023): www.nato.int/cps/en/natolive/news_72931.htm%3FselectedLocale%3Den.

Japan's political leadership have also engaged with NATO, such as Prime Minister Fumio Kishida's participation in the 2022 NATO Summit in Madrid. Some of these dynamics reflect NATO and its democratic partners' response to growing Chinese power. Outgroup threat is, after all, a way to spur ingroup solidarity. While serving a strategic purpose, these partnerships are solidified by their shared identity and norms. For example, a joint statement by NATO Secretary General Jens Stoltenberg and PM Kishida characterized the relationship as being between "natural partners who share common values of freedom, democracy, and the rule of law, as well as strategic interests."[150]

These state-level politics have seeped down to the domestic level as well. Japanese public discourse and opinion often feature the country's relations with the United States, including on matters of U.S. military intervention, as well as its dealings with the Security Council and NATO. Two pieces of data verify this claim. First, the content of Japanese newspapers reveals that U.S. intervention and IOs are salient in Japan. Table 3 summarizes the number of Japanese news article headlines that include the search terms United States, UNSC, and NATO, along with the benchmark terms WTO and SDF.[151] It shows that the country's top liberal and conservative newspapers, the Asahi and Yomiuri Shimbun, reported substantially on relevant topics in the six-month windows surrounding episodes of U.S. military intervention across three different U.S. presidencies: March 1999 Kosovo (Clinton); March 2003 Iraq (Bush); and March 2011 Libya (Obama). In 1999 Kosovo, when the United States intervened with NATO without Security Council authorization, newspapers reported more about NATO than the Security Council and its military (347 versus 179 headlines). Surrounding the Iraq invasion, the United States received a high degree of attention for its unilateralism (726 headlines). The Security Council and NATO played a more equal role in Libya, as reflected in their roughly equal coverage. Overall, the United States was the most salient topic, and the Security Council and NATO were more frequently reported upon than the WTO and sometimes even the SDF.

Second, the Japanese public holds meaningful knowledge of NATO and the UN, as demonstrated by opinion polls summarized in Table 4A–B. A panel of twenty-four surveys conducted online monthly from October 2011 to September 2013 by researchers at Waseda University shows that about

[150] Source (accessed April 11, 2023): https://japan.kantei.go.jp/content/000122397.pdf. More broadly, Chu, Ko, and Liu (2021) show that social, value-based rhetoric builds support for alliances.

[151] To ensure that the term is a substantial article topic, the data counts *headlines* instead of articles that mention the search term anywhere.

Table 3 Japanese news during armed interventions by three different U.S. presidents

Search Term	Jan to June 1999 Kosovo, Clinton		Jan to June 2003 Iraq, Bush		Jan to June 2011 Libya, Obama		Total
	Asahi	**Yomiuri**	**Asahi**	**Yomiuri**	**Asahi**	**Yomiuri**	
U.S.	436 (38%)	477 (44%)	726 (6%)	581 (58%)	251 (50%)	153 (37%)	2,624 (49%)
Security Council	72 (6%)	55 (5%)	161 (13%)	176 (18%)	21 (4%)	24 (6%)	509 (10%)
NATO	347 (30%)	330 (31%)	25 (2%)	37 (4%)	31 (6%)	34 (8%)	804 (15%)
WTO	110 (10%)	93 (9%)	69 (6%)	57 (6%)	8 (2%)	12 (3%)	349 (7%)
SDF	179 (16%)	118 (11%)	227 (19%)	148 (15%)	195 (39%)	196 (47%)	1063 (20%)
Total	1144	1073	1208	999	506	419	5349

Note: The numbers represent the count and (column-wise percentages) of headlines that include certain search terms. From top to bottom, the Japanese search terms for the headlines were "アメリカ OR 米国"; "国連安全保障理事会 OR 安保理"; "NATO OR ナトー OR 北大西洋条約機構"; "WTO OR 世界貿易機関"; "自衛 OR 自衛隊". The searches were conducted using the *Asahi Kikuzo II Visual* and the *Yomidasu Rekishikan (databases)*.

Table 4A Japanese knowledge of NATO

Q: Which IO is called by the abbreviation NATO?	
Answer Choices	Min to max percentage across surveys
An organization ...	
To protect the environment of the Arctic	3.7 to 5.5
To promote free trade on the North American continent	16.3 to 20.2
A military alliance among the US, Canada, and major European countries	59.7 to 65.1
To promote cultural exchange between South and North America	0.7 to 1.5
Don't Know	12.4 to 15.7
Sample Size	2,071 to 3,481

Note: The answer choice order was randomized, except for "Don't Know," which was always given last. The data are from a 2011–2013 monthly panel survey. The table reports the minimum to maximum range across twenty-four surveys. Data are from the "Survey on the Image of Foreign Countries and Current Topics," Research Institute of Contemporary Japanese Systems at Waseda University, which are archived at and available from the Institute of Social Science, University of Tokyo.

Table 4B Japanese knowledge of the UN

Q: Where is the current United Nations Secretary General from?	
Answer Choices	Min to max percentage across surveys
USA	4.2 to 5.9
People's Republic of China	3.1 to 6.3
Ghana	5.7 to 8.5
South Korea	56.9 to 61.7
Don't Know	21.8 to 26.4
Sample Size	2,071 to 3,481

Note: Ibid.

60–65 percent of survey takers correctly identified NATO as an IO enshrining a military alliance among the United States, Canada, and European countries. It also finds that about 55–60 percent of the respondents knew that the UN Secretary-General was from South Korea at the time (Ban Ki Moon). The correct choices were randomized among three reasonable but incorrect answers, and respondents were allowed to select "Don't Know."[152] These results indicate that Japanese citizens are reasonably knowledgeable of the UN and NATO.

The salience of IOs and U.S. intervention in Japanese society is politically relevant because Japanese public opinion affects the country's foreign policy. While other domestic actors like the bureaucracy and media are influential,[153] Japanese citizens still matter to foreign policymaking in their own right.[154] In an extensive study of the public's impact on foreign policy since the end of WWII, Paul Midford concludes that "Japanese public opinion is influential because it is stable, coherent, and, regarding beliefs about the utility of military force, not easily or quickly swayed by elite attempts to influence it."[155] Other research further finds that Japanese citizens tend to be a "conservative" force on statecraft, constraining policy-makers from pursuing more militaristic actions such as contributing to U.S. military operations.[156] These findings about Japan are consistent with research more generally showing how public opinion exerts democratic pressures on governments.[157]

Thus, overall, Japan and Japanese public opinion are relevant and responsive to the broader foreign policies of liberal democracies, including the involvement of IOs. This case background demonstrates that cues from IOs like NATO can plausibly reach foreign audiences like the Japanese public, which establishes the real-world relevance of the subsequent experimental analyses. Lastly, international relations research often overlooks East Asian cases,[158] and this shortcoming is especially relevant to testing my social cues argument. Specifically, investigating Japanese public opinion helps to confront questions about whether the liberal community and NATO's influence reflect a Western identity versus a broader democratic identity.[159] If the patterns found in American opinion do not replicate in Japan, we should be less confident that the "liberal community" extends beyond the West. Studying Japan answers these critical questions.

5.1.2 Japan Survey: Methodology

I commissioned Nikkei Research to conduct two national surveys in Japan.[160] Nikkei fielded the first survey in March 2015 to 12,233 respondents[161] and

[152] For NATO, incorrect choices are an organization to protect the environment, to promote North American free trade, and to promote South and North American cultural exchange. For the UNSC, incorrect choices are USA, China, and Ghana.
[153] Johnson 1975; Shinoda 2007.
[154] Risse-Kappen 1991, 508–509; Katzenstein 2008, 19.
[155] Midford 2011, 7.
[156] Bobrow 1989; Berger 2003; Midford 2006.
[157] E.g. Aldrich et al. 2006; Baum and Potter 2015; Tomz, Weeks, and Yarhi-Milo 2020; Chu and Recchia 2022.
[158] Johnston 2012.
[159] E.g., Hemmer and Katzenstein 2002; Vucetic 2011.
[160] See the Online Appendix for the survey text in Japanese and its translation in English.
[161] Due to a technical error, Nikkei Research collected more respondents than the targeted 2,000 respondents. This error did not affect the experimental procedures in the survey.

the second replication survey in December 2015 to 3,587 respondents. Nikkei administered the survey online and used stratified random sampling procedures to meet demographic and geographic targets based on the *Jūminkihondaichō* (Basic Resident Register). Because both surveys replicated the same substantive results, their data are combined in the following results. The disaggregated results are in the Online Appendix.

Both surveys included a vignette-based experiment similar to the one used in the U.S. surveys described in Section 2. However, the Japanese scenario was about a U.S. humanitarian intervention rather than an intervention conducted by the respondent's country, Japan. To review, the survey vignette contained three main sections. First, it described (in Japanese) a humanitarian crisis emerging from a civil war in a foreign country. Second, it randomized information about whether NATO and the Security Council opposed or endorsed a U.S. humanitarian intervention in the crisis (*Both Oppose, NATO Only, UNSC Only, Both Support*). To test the hypothesis about whether social cues are stronger when institutionalized, it also independently randomized information about the cue-sender: whether both the IO and its member countries were named, or just the IO or the member countries. Lastly, after explaining that the United States took military action under one of the four main experimental conditions, respondents were asked to express their approval of the U.S. military operations.

5.1.3 Effect of Social Cues on Japanese Public Opinion

The results of the two Japanese surveys replicate the main findings from the U.S. study. First, as Figure 12 reports, NATO's policy endorsement affects Japanese support for U.S. humanitarian intervention more strongly than the Security Council. As the left-side figure shows, a sole Security Council cue increases public approval: the increase from *Both Oppose* to *UNSC Only* is about 7 percentage points (pp.). However, the more explicit ingroup cue by NATO raises support by a larger amount. The increase from *Both Oppose* to *NATO Only* is about 16 pp. Furthermore, obtaining the approval of both IOs does not significantly change public approval above and beyond just obtaining the approval of NATO (comparing *NATO Only* to *Both Endorse*). Turning to the right-side figure, the analysis also shows that the average NATO treatment effect is about 9 pp. higher than the average Security Council treatment effect. As with the U.S. surveys, the fact that the Security Council has a negligible effect conditional on receiving the ingroup cue from NATO, but not the reverse, cannot be easily explained by existing rational information theories.

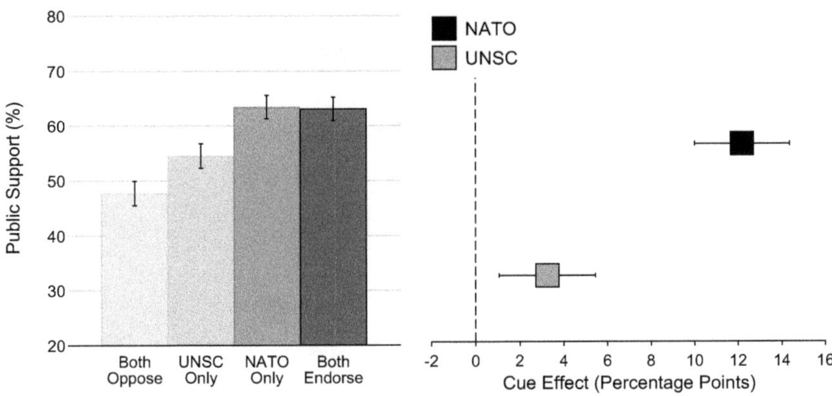

Figure 12 NATO has a greater effect than the Security Council (Japan). The figure on the left shows public approval of U.S. intervention in four scenarios regarding NATO and the Security Council's stance on intervention. The figure on the right reports the average treatment effect of each IO. 95% confidence intervals are displayed. $N = 7{,}852$. Data are from Survey JPN-1 & JPN-2.

Next, the results reported in Figure 13 show that the liberal community is more influential when sending its social cues through NATO. Specifically, the liberal community's endorsement effect is about 3 pp. greater when channeled through NATO (comparing the top two estimates). While the effect size is modest, it is statistically significant and replicates the findings from the U.S. study. Next, due to the greater number of observations available in the Japan surveys, I could assess the effect of institutionalized cues from the broader international community, as represented by the Security Council. My theory argues that institutions can clarify the social meaning of a cue, but the international community does not represent any specific social group. Indeed, as Figure 13 shows, institutionalizing the international community's endorsement vis-à-vis the Security Council does not change its effect on Japanese public opinion (comparing the bottom two estimates). Thus, institutionalized social cues are especially influential; institutionalized cues from no particular social group are not.

5.1.4 Generalizability of the Japan Case

Japan is a policy-relevant case suitable for theory testing and is thus intrinsically valuable to study. Still, researchers might wonder how the results speak to other countries. While countries differ on countless dimensions, Japan would likely be a middling case regarding the effect of IO cues on public approval for at least two reasons. First, there are cross-cutting forces in modern Japan–U.S. relations.

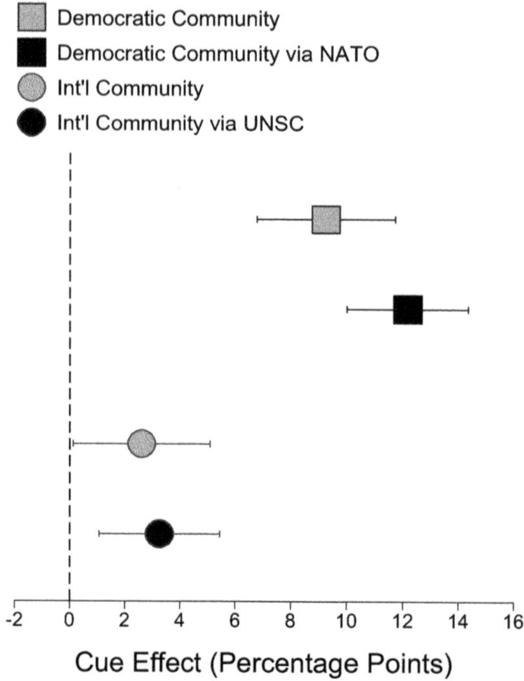

Figure 13 The effect of institutionalized cues (Japan). This figure shows the effect of the democratic community, the broader international community, and their cues sent through NATO or the Security Council on public opinion. $N = 7{,}852$. Data are from Survey JPN-1 & JPN-2.

Japan is a close liberal democratic ally of the United States that generally expresses affinity with Americans, which could make its citizens more trusting of the United States and thus less interested in obtaining an external endorsement from an IO. It is also, however, anti-militaristic and wary of entrapment by overly hawkish U.S. policies, which could make its citizens especially interested in hearing what an institutional institution thinks.[162] Japan is thus not a clear case for being particularly susceptible or immune to the cues of IOs.

Second, Japanese beliefs about whether the United States has a positive or negative impact on the international system (which approximates their potential concerns about U.S. military intervention) are close to the average of dozens of other countries. In a 2010–11 BBC World Service Poll, the difference in percentages of Japanese who believed the United States to be a positive versus negative influence in the world was 25 pp., compared to an average of 18 pp. among twenty-five other countries representing various regions and regime

[162] Izumikawa 2010, 129–132.

types.[163] Countries more pessimistic about the United States, like Germany (−7 pp.) and China (−20 pp.), might value an IO's authorization even more than Japan. In contrast, countries with more optimistic views about the United States, like Italy (38 pp.) and South Korea (55 pp.), will presumably care less about an IO's second opinion.

Overall, the Japan study demonstrates that social cues by the liberal community and NATO affect foreign public opinion as they affect domestic opinion in the United States. Furthermore, because Japan is an Asian liberal democracy, this evidence challenges claims about how the liberal community effect is restricted to the "West." These results are likely generalizable to other contexts, which I will explore in the following section.

5.2 Foreign Elites: A Survey of UK Parliamentarians

Social cues influence not just everyday citizens but also political elites. After all, elites are also social beings who care about norms, group belonging, and status. In fact, political elites might be expected to be even *more* conscientious about their country's adherence to international norms and standing among peer nations compared to everyday citizens who are preoccupied with bread-and-butter issues. Indeed, existing research about social identity dynamics in international relations emphasizes state and elite-level dynamics.[164] Earlier arguments about the signaling effects of IOs also highlighted the role of foreign elites.[165]

I examine political elites by surveying members of parliament (MPs) in the United Kingdom House of Commons.[166] The United Kingdom is a critical player in the politics of humanitarian intervention, and its MPs are often directly involved in high-level policymaking, including holding relevant cabinet minister positions. Specifically, I contracted YouGov to poll a representative sample of 103 MPs.[167] YouGov's fieldwork took place in March and April 2023. While it was not possible to conduct a survey experiment on the MPs,[168] I did survey a representative sample of them on a question relevant to the social cue theory. The question was the following:

> *In a given situation, international organizations might disagree on whether humanitarian intervention should be allowed. In which of the following two*

---

[163] The complete list is available in the Online Appendix.

[164] Johnston 2008; Checkel and Katzenstein 2009. [165] Voeten 2005; Thompson 2009.

[166] See Chu and Recchia (2022) for the first published use of this sample in political science.

[167] YouGov conducts targeted sampling and then applies post-sample weights on respondent party, gender, electoral cohort, and geography to give a sample that is representative of the House of Commons.

[168] Specifically, the maximum sample size was 100 and would not generate sufficient power for my experimental design. Furthermore, YouGov's reputation team ensures long-term relations with the elite sample, which restricts deception and certain types of experiments.

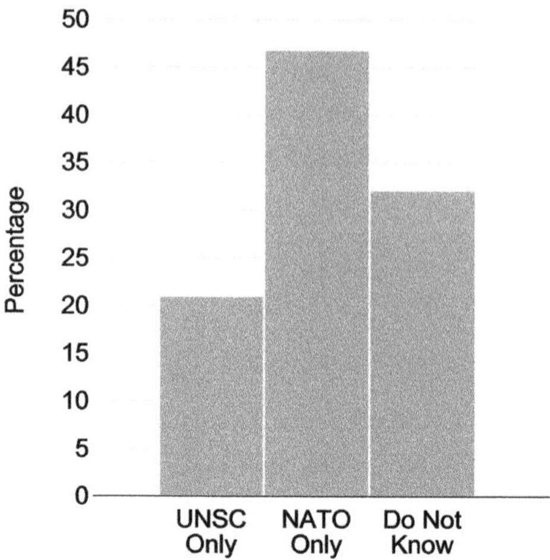

Figure 14 When forced to choose, UK MPs prefer intervention with NATO over the Security Council. This figure shows the percentage of MPs in the UK Parliament who would rather support humanitarian with the Security Council but not NATO's endorsement (UNSC Only) versus NATO but not the Security Council's endorsement (NATO Only), or stated they "Don't know." $N = 103$. Data from Survey UK-MP.

situations would you personally be more likely to support humanitarian intervention? We understand that in reality there are many factors to consider, but we'd just like to hear your general intuition.

- The Security Council approves of an intervention, but NATO has refrained from giving its endorsement due to the opposition of key NATO members.
- NATO approves of an intervention, but the Security Council has refrained from giving its endorsement due to the opposition of key Security Council members.
- Don't Know.

In essence, this question asks respondents to compare policy options that mirror the *UNSC Only* and *NATO Only* prompts from the experimental studies. The social cue theory predicts that the MPs would favor NATO approval without the Security Council over the reverse because NATO approval represents a clearer ingroup cue. Figure 14 summarizes the results of this survey question and confirms the social cue theory's prediction. Twenty-one percent of the MPs prefer humanitarian intervention with the Security Council but not NATO's approval, while 47 percent prefer NATO but not Security Council approval. That is a 26 pp. difference.

While this statistic alone cannot be interpreted as causal or revealing *why* such preference exists, it does help to triangulate an additional dimension of the social cue theory in conjunction with other parts of this Element. We can also look to secondary historical evidence to corroborate NATO's social impact on elites. For example, Gheciu (2005) shows how Romania's entry into NATO socialized its policymakers to become amenable to liberal democratic rhetorical frames and policy arguments. This socialization process ultimately led Romanian lawmakers to accept arguments by the West regarding how Europe should address the 1999 Kosovo conflict. Thus, the survey shows that MPs in the United Kingdom generally prioritize NATO's endorsement over the Security Council's, and existing research documents social dynamics emanating from NATO to policymakers in other contexts.

5.3 Egypt, Outside the Liberal Community

To test some final implications of the social theory, I conducted a survey experiment outside the democratic context: Egypt. The Egypt survey mirrors the U.S. and Japanese surveys, except it simultaneously presented Egyptian survey takers with the policy position of *three* different IOs: the Security Council, NATO, and the Arab League. So, each IO was independently randomized to either approve or disapprove of humanitarian intervention, creating six different experimental conditions. Like the Japan survey, the dependent variable is support for U.S. humanitarian intervention. The survey was fielded by Qualtrics in Arabic to a diverse sample of 1,839 Egyptians.

The social cue theory implies that people will care first and foremost about ingroup cues. Thus, in the aggregate, the Arab League's cue should have the most substantial effect on Egyptians because it represents an Arabic regional and cultural identity. NATO may also affect Egyptian mass opinion if some respondents identify with the liberal community, perhaps due to Egypt's recent struggles for democracy, especially after the Arab Spring. But this prediction is less concrete ex ante. Lastly, the Security Council may or may not affect Egyptian public opinion. If it does, it would be for reasons outside the social cue logic.

The data are consistent with the argument that only ingroup cues influence mass policy preferences in Egypt. Figure 15 shows that neither NATO nor the Security Council shifts Egyptian approval to a statistically significant degree. However, the Arab League's policy endorsement significantly increases Egyptian approval of U.S. humanitarian intervention by almost 6 pp. While this analysis does not assess causal mediators to explain the main experimental effects, it does show how the logic of ingroup cues operates in a different context than the liberal democratic community.

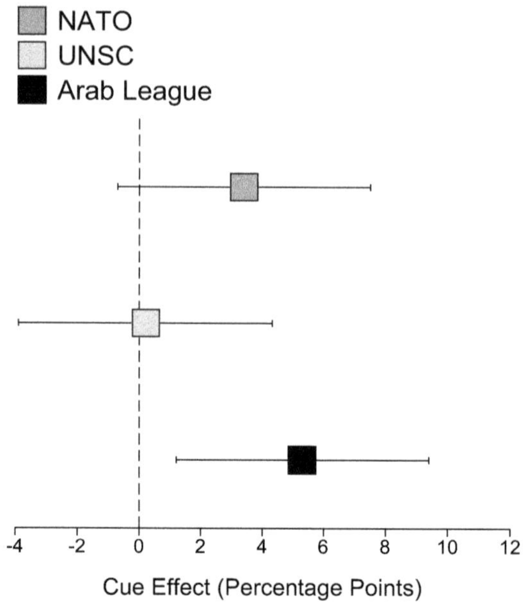

Figure 15 In Egypt, only the Arab League's cue significantly affects public opinion. This figure shows the effect of each IO, averaging across the possible conditions of the other two IOs, on public approval of U.S. intervention. $N = 1{,}839$. Data are from Survey EGY.

6 Reassessing the Literature

The preceding sections provide strong evidence for this Element's central claim: the liberal community and NATO can send social cues that legitimize humanitarian war among both domestic and international audiences. While any single finding in isolation might be open to alternative explanations, only the social cue theory explains the broad range of empirical patterns as a cohesive whole.

At the same time, these findings raise questions for existing theories on the Security Council's role. While the social cue perspective was not initially presented as mutually exclusive with these theories, the data reveal some tension. The prevailing view has been that the Security Council exerts a legitimizing force on public attitudes toward war. The absence of Security Council authorization may not entirely delegitimize war, but its explicit approval is generally assumed to wield substantial influence. I address this tension in two ways. First, I revisit previous empirical findings that were interpreted as supporting conventional wisdom, demonstrating how they can align with the social cue theory. Then, I present new analyses to directly evaluate potential counterarguments from the legal and rational information transmission perspectives.

6.1 Reframing Existing Evidence

Existing evidence has been interpreted as demonstrating the Security Council's importance in granting legal legitimacy and in transmitting information about the material outcomes of war. How can we reconcile such interpretations with this study? In theory, both NATO and the Security Council could exert influence, albeit for different reasons. Additionally, as the Security Council includes key leaders from the democratic community, it may exert a social cue effect, though perhaps in a more diluted form. However, the evidence presented in this Element does not support these interpretations. Furthermore, upon closer scrutiny, previous studies can also be reinterpreted as being consistent with the social cue theory or at least inconclusive in differentiating between the competing explanations.

To begin, studies using historical data to examine the effect of international organizations (IOs) on public opinion have proven inconclusive, as there is limited historical variation in the institutional design and membership of these IOs.[169] The Security Council has consistently held its role as the sole legal authority on war, governed by an elite pact, and structured as an independent, diverse, and conservative institution. This continuity provides little to no observational variation to test the mechanisms (i.e., elite pact, independence, etc.) proposed by existing theories. Additionally, cases in which NATO and the Security Council explicitly disagree are rare, further limiting the historical data's ability to illuminate cross-institutional differences. From a social scientific perspective, these limitations make it challenging to use historical data alone to evaluate which institutions – and what institutional properties – truly matter.

Recognizing these limitations, some studies have turned to experimental data from public opinion surveys, as does this study. Two existing experimental studies could be interpreted as supporting conventional wisdom, but upon closer examination, one can be consistent with both conventional perspectives and the social cue theory, while the other provides direct support for the social cue theory. First, Grieco et al. (2011) conducted a national survey experiment in the United States via telephone, finding that the joint endorsement of NATO and the Security Council raises American approval by approximately 24–27 percentage points (pp.). This effect mirrors the roughly 30 pp. effect I discovered in Survey USA-1 when comparing *Both Oppose* with *Both Endorse*, as discussed in Section 3. However, as Grieco et al (2011) randomized both IOs simultaneously, it does not measure each IO's independent effects.

[169] Hainmueller, Mummolo, and Xu (2019, 25–28) make this observation.

Second, Tago and Ikeda (2015) tested Japanese public approval for U.S. military action under four conditions: (1) unanimous Security Council approval, (2) Security Council approval with abstentions by Russia and China and four nonpermanent members voting no, (3) lack of Security Council approval due to a veto by Russia and China, and (4) no attempt to seek Security Council approval due to anticipated opposition. While public support was higher in the first three conditions than in the fourth, support levels among those first three conditions were indistinguishable from one another. The authors interpreted this as an "A for effort" effect, suggesting that governments receive public approval mainly for attempting to secure Security Council authorization. However, social cue theory offers an alternative interpretation: Japanese approval increases so long as the United States secures the approval of democratic allies like the UK and France, while opposition from outgroup countries such as China and Russia is discounted. With these studies reconsidered through the lens of the social cue theory, I now directly reexamine additional claims made by the conventional theories.

6.2 Reexamining Legal Theories

One existing perspective argues that institutions legitimize armed interventions by legalizing them. To elaborate, since the creation of the United Nations, international law bans international wars with only three exceptions: self-defense, collective self-defense, and uses of force authorized by the Security Council.[170] Under this system, the Security Council has broad authority to legalize the use of armed force to address, as a last resort, threats to international peace and security. Over time, the Security Council has expanded its mandate to authorize military interventions in humanitarian crises. Procedurally, the Security Council does this by passing a "Chapter VII" resolution, which requires nine of the fifteen members' affirmative votes and no dissenting votes from the permanent five members, China, France, Russia, the United Kingdom, and the United States. Under this doctrine, ad hoc coalitions and alternative IOs like NATO do not have the same authority to legalize war.

International law could change how people think about war for several reasons. A Security Council resolution could convince people that a crisis poses a "threat to international peace and security" that can only be addressed via a military operation. But even if people are unfamiliar with the Security Council's technical mandate, they could more generally prefer legal policies over illegal ones. This preference could be for normative reasons, as people worldwide favor legality, especially those residing in countries with a legalistic

[170] Frank 2002.

culture that respects the rule of law.[171] But such a preference could also be for more instrumental reasons. For example, Guzman (2008) finds that abiding by the law helps to avoid reciprocity, reputation costs, and retaliation.[172] Thus, the Security Council could grant "legal legitimacy" to armed intervention,[173] which could attract supporters for these various normative and instrumental reasons.

The previous sections showed how the Security Council, the only institution with the authority to legalize humanitarian war, exerts a modest influence on domestic and international opinion. This finding challenges the legal perspective, though proponents of this view may still raise two critiques regarding the analysis.

First, the aggregate mass public lacks an appreciation for the importance of international law, as most people are not well-informed about it.[174] To address this critique, I demonstrate that the effect of IOs on public opinion is similar regardless of respondents' understanding of international law. In Survey USA-1, respondents were asked: "Under international law, which of the following organizations do you think can authorize the use of military force in another country? Please select all that apply." The response options were the following: United Nations Security Council, North Atlantic Treaty Organization (NATO), International Court of Justice (ICJ), Global Military Council, and None of the above.[175] I categorized the respondents into "Know Law" and "Don't Know Law" groups based on whether they correctly identified the Security Council as the sole authorizing body. Less than a quarter of respondents (237 out of 1,000) fell into the "Know Law" category.

Using this data, I examine whether respondents' knowledge of international law influences how they respond to cues from the Security Council and NATO. Figure 16 reveals no such influence. Even those who correctly identified the Security Council as the sole legal authority remain susceptible to NATO's social cues (as seen in the shift from *Both Oppose* to *NATO Only* along the solid line). While knowledge of international law slightly reduces public support for interventions lacking Security Council approval (indicated by the lower

[171] Chong 1993; Koh 1997; Finnemore and Sikkink 1998; Goodman and Jinks 2013; Hafner-Burton, LeVeck, and Victor 2016.

[172] For evidence on how international law shapes public opinion via the reputation mechanism, see Tomz 2008.

[173] Tago 2005, 589; Tago and Ikeda 2015, 392.

[174] Note, however, that the legal theories do not require the public to explicitly know the technicalities of international law to be influenced by it. Norm internalization can begin at the institutional level (i.e., international law), but then political elites and transnational actors might transmit the norm to ordinary citizens without transmitting the particular legal knowledge.

[175] These response options were presented in randomized order, except "None of the above" that always appeared last. "Global Security Council" was a red herring.

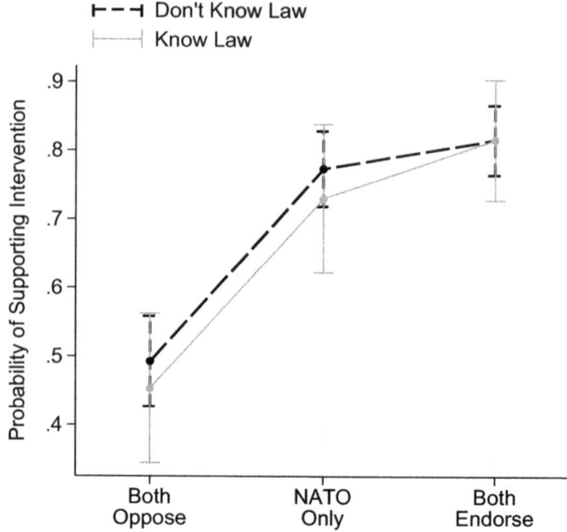

Figure 16 Beliefs about international law do not moderate NATO's Influence. Using probit coefficient estimates, this figure shows the predicted probability of supporting intervention for each treatment group, conditional on whether respondents know international law ($N = 237$) or do not ($N = 763$). Those who "Know Law" correctly identified the UNSC as the sole IO that can authorize interventions. 95% confidence intervals are displayed. These data are from Survey USA-1.

position of the solid line compared to the dotted line across *Both Oppose* and *NATO Only*), this reduction is modest at best.

A second critique might argue that the true impact of international law on public opinion only emerges when respondents are directly informed about legal requirements. This perspective suggests an "out of sight, out of mind" effect for international law or implies that the law's influence primarily manifests through public discourse, enabling political opponents to argue that a country has violated international law if it acts without Security Council approval. If this critique holds, NATO's endorsement should have less impact on respondents' approval when they are *explicitly informed* that Security Council approval is legally required. Specifically, informing people that a humanitarian intervention requires Security Council authorization should diminish NATO's independent effect on public opinion.

I test this hypothesis using data from Survey USA-4. In this survey, I independently randomize (1) whether respondents receive the *Both Oppose* or the *NATO Only* scenario and (2) whether respondents receive an explicit statement about international law. All respondents read: "The United States is

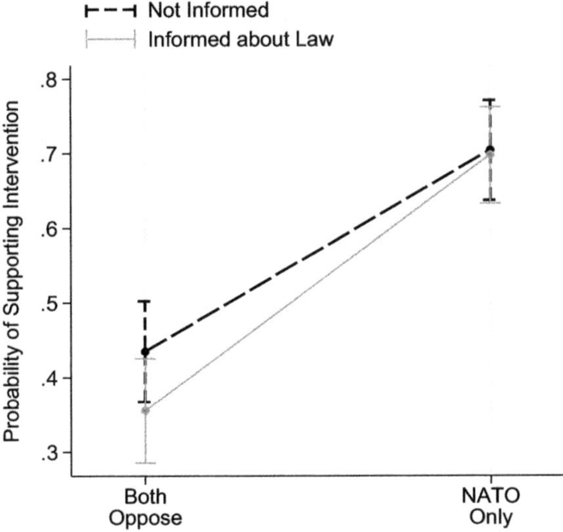

Figure 17 Explicit information about international law does not suppress NATO's influence. Using probit coefficient estimates, this figure shows the predicted probability of supporting intervention for each treatment group, conditional on whether respondents are (experimentally) informed about international law (*N* = 375) or not (*N* = 386). 95% confidence intervals are displayed. The data are from Survey USA-4.

considering taking military action to help civilians in this crisis." Respondents selected to receive the explicit statement about international law additionally read: "To be legal under international law, taking military action in this situation requires United Nations Security Council authorization." Figure 17 visualizes the results, showing that NATO approval increases public support for intervention regardless of whether respondents were informed about international law (dotted or solid line).

However, providing legal information does reduce public approval in scenarios where both NATO and the Security Council oppose intervention. When respondents are informed of international law's requirements, they are less supportive of the *Both Oppose* condition, suggesting that knowledge of legal standards increases sensitivity to Security Council disapproval – but only when NATO also disapproves. Once NATO endorses intervention, legal concerns largely disappear from consideration. This finding aligns with other research suggesting that international law influences public opinion primarily when it aligns with deeper norms and values. For example, Chu (2019) shows that international humanitarian law restrains public support for torturing enemy prisoners of war only if the opposing country also respects such laws; otherwise, support for torture remains unaffected by legal prohibitions. Similarly, Bayram (2017) demonstrates that the impact of international law depends on respondents already holding cosmopolitan values. Thus, international law often reinforces preexisting norms, values, and identities – such as reciprocity and cosmopolitanism – rather than independently shaping public opinion.

6.3 Reexamining Rational Information Transmission Theories

I now turn to rational information transmission theories. Because there are several strands of this theory, I will first outline their key arguments before presenting additional analyses to evaluate them. These theories generally suggest that the Security Council, due to its unique institutional properties, conveys critical information about the costs, benefits, and likely consequences of military action through its policy endorsements.

One version of this argument views the Security Council as an "elite pact" whose approval can reassure foreign governments and citizens about the consequences of using military force.[176] Specifically, Security Council authorization signals that military intervention will not lead to great power conflict or destabilize the international system, which can mitigate opposition to intervention. The Security Council's distinctive attributes contribute to this perceived reassurance. First, its foundation as an institution brokered by post-WWII great powers means its decisions reflect the will of major players in global affairs. Second, the Council's history of checking powerful states, including the United States, has established it as a credible institution for coordinating global security. Consequently, as some scholars have argued, the Security Council is "a more viable candidate than alternative institutions,"[177] including NATO.[178]

A second perspective within the rational information transmission theories posits that *independent or neutral* IOs are best suited to relay useful information to observers.[179] Drawing from formal models on the informational role of legislative committees,[180] this perspective argues that IOs with a more heterogeneous or diverse set of veto players are more independent and, therefore, more influential. The logic here is that if such a diverse group of countries can agree on a policy, people will perceive such a policy as producing good consequences or at least not harmful. Focusing on how the Security Council, Thompson (2009) notes that "in security matters, the Security Council … comes closest to operating as a neutral representative of the international community in a case of military intervention" and that "this logic helps explain why regional organizations, comprised of a less diverse set of states, do not

[176] Voeten 2005, 528. [177] Voeten 2005, 547. [178] Voeten 2005, 541–542.
[179] Thompson 2009; Bush and Prather 2018. [180] Krehbiel 1991.

produce a legitimation effect equivalent to that of the Security Council," including "the more parochial NATO."[181]

A final related argument holds that the policy positions of *conservative* IOs provide the most informative signal to observers.[182] Conservative IOs, which rarely endorse military intervention or pose a "high legislative hurdle" to war, are seen as more credible when they do support it. In such cases, the "legislative hurdle" often stems from a pivotal voting member with dovish preferences or preferences that deviate most substantially from the intervening party.[183] Therefore, when such a conservative IO endorses war, observers should be more likely to conclude that war would produce favorable outcomes. Again, this line of argument predicts that the Security Council's blessing can raise support for war, especially in the case of humanitarian intervention, where veto-holders like China and Russia hold conservative preferences relative to the liberal community.[184] In contrast, policy endorsements from more hawkish IOs that do not pose as high of a hurdle to authorization, like NATO, should be in an inferior position to relay helpful information. The logic is that if a warmongering institution supports war, it does not say much about whether war is a good idea.

The evidence thus far, however, already contrasts with these expectations. Sections 3 and 5 show that the Security Council had little impact once people in the United States and Japan received an ingroup endorsement from NATO. UK policymakers even preferred an intervention backed solely by NATO over one backed solely by the Security Council. Moreover, Section 4 employed a variety of research designs to show that the institutional cues are not operating through the logic of shaping people's expectations about material outcomes. Thus, the Security Council's endorsements are not consistently influential, nor can the domestic influence of IOs be entirely explained by people's attempts to glean information about war's material cost and benefits.

Based on this discussion, I evaluate three potential defenses for the rational information transmission theories. The first defense is another political ignorance critique, suggesting that much of the public does not hold "correct" perceptions about the Security Council and NATO. So, the problem is not with the theory but whether the theory generalizes to a largely ignorant public. Several pieces of evidence from previous sections contradict this argument. Specifically, the politically engaged public responds to the cue of IOs in ways that resemble the mass public: college-educated Americans who are registered to vote and frequently follow international political news respond to ingroup

[181] Thompson 2009, 37–38. [182] Chapman 2011. [183] Chapman 2011, Chapter 2.

[184] This perspective is at tension with Tago and Ikeda's (2015) finding regarding how the Security Council affects Japanese opinion even with a Russian and Chinese veto, as discussed earlier.

cues perhaps even more acutely than the mass public (discussed in Section 3 and reported in the Online Appendix). This result also aligns with the finding reported in Section 5 about the UK MPs, who are knowledgeable policy elites that should be likely to "correctly" perceive the Security Council's institutional properties.

A second defense might be that there are just too many differences between NATO and the Security Council to isolate the effect of these specific institutional properties on public attitudes. Section 4 presented several pieces of evidence to show that NATO's effect can be attributed to social cueing; however, these findings are not necessarily direct negative evidence for the alternative mechanisms relating to institutional independence and conservativeness.

Here, I directly analyze the rational informational transmission theories' central assumptions about independence and conservativeness, which existing approaches operationalize using the diversity and distance of preferences of an institution's member countries.[185] Specifically, in the second Japan survey, I measured each respondent's beliefs about a selection of NATO and the Security Council's key member countries in terms of whether respondents believed that key members from each IO are committed to human rights (norms) and, alternatively, politically aligned with Japan (strategic).[186] The individual responses were then used to calculate an independence score (i.e., the heterogeneity/diversity of ratings, as measured by the variance of ratings), and a conservative score (i.e., the most distant rating or "highest legislative hurdle," using the strategic measure only). For space, the Online Appendix discusses these research procedures in greater detail.

The results are clear. As summarized in Table 5, the general public perceives the Security Council as far more independent and conservative than NATO. Thus, the Security Council's overall weak cue effect cannot be explained by mass ignorance about its institutional properties. To delve deeper, using multivariate regression analysis for individual-level analysis, I estimated how perceiving each IO as independent or conservative affects the ability of that IO to change people's support for humanitarian intervention. As summarized in the final row of Table 6, the interaction coefficient *IO*Property* (which can be either independence or conservativeness) is generally positive, as the

[185] Thompson (2009, 34) operationalizes institutional independence (or neutrality) using the diversity or heterogeneity of its membership. Research studies measure an IO's conservativeness using the *distance* between an IO's pivotal member and the cue recipient (Chapman 2011, 51–56). See also Section 5 for a specific discussion about foreign public opinion.

[186] Asking respondents to rate each IO's *complete* membership may have been preferable but overly costly and taxing. The set of countries thus include two countries exclusive to the Security Council (China and Russia), two countries exclusive to NATO (Canada and Germany), and one that is in both (the UK).

Table 5 Japanese perceive the Security Council to be more independent and conservative than NATO

	Percentage of people perceiving the IO as . . .		
	Independent (Norms)	Independent (Strategic)	Conservative (Strategic)
Security Council			
Not at all	16%	24%	11%
Somewhat	44%	55%	34%
Very	40%	21%	55%
NATO			
Not at all	69%	71%	56%
Somewhat	30%	28%	39%
Very	1%	1%	5%

Note: For each IO, the sum of percentages among Not at all, Somewhat, and Very is about 100, with a rounding error. $N = 3{,}587$. Data are from Survey JPN-2.

conventional wisdom would predict. That is, viewing the Security Council or NATO as more independent or conservative amplifies the effect of its cues on public opinion. However, the size of that effect is substantively small, and it is also statistically indistinguishable from having zero effect.

The third potential defense is that IOs are intended to influence only a specific subset of people – namely, those who are skeptical of an intervening country's political motives and concerned about the potential consequences of war for the international system.[187] According to this view, the Security Council's legitimizing effect should be most potent among individuals who perceive the interventionist country as reckless or imprudent in international affairs. If IOs serve this reassurance function, then those who doubt the intervening country's reliability and restraint most strongly should be most responsive to Security Council endorsements.

I test this argument regarding the effect of IOs among war-weary citizens, again using data from the Japanese public opinion on U.S. intervention. The survey takers answered the question, "Do you agree or disagree with the following statement: 'The U.S. generally makes good decisions about using military force in other countries.'" Depending on their answers, respondents were grouped into three categories: those who agreed, those who neither agreed nor disagreed, and those who disagreed. These three groups were labeled as those who believe the United States to be *Prudent*, *Neutral*, or *Imprudent*.

187 Voeten 2005; Fang 2008; Thompson 2009; Chapman 2011.

Table 6 Perceptions of independence and conservativeness do not moderate IO effects

	Property = Independent (Norms)		*Property* = Independent (Strategic)		*Property* = Conservative (Strategic)	
Independent Variables	*UNSC*	*NATO*	*UNSC*	*NATO*	*UNSC*	*NATO*
IO Endorsement	0.016	**0.152**	0.019	**0.122**	0.002	**0.170**
Property^{IO}	0.074	0.040	**0.078**	−0.025	0.034	−0.065
*IO***Property*	0.061	−0.043	0.066	0.048	0.086	−0.074

Note: This table reports the marginal effects from four separate probit regressions, conditional on other variables being held at their means. The dependent variable is Approval, which takes the value of 1 if the respondent approves of U.S. intervention and 0 if they disapprove. The following control variables can be found in the Online Appendix: gender, age, education, ideology, voting status, cosmopolitanism, isolationism, and exceptionalism. The null effect of *IO**Property does not depend on the inclusion of control variables. Estimates significant at the 0.05 level are in bold. $N = 1{,}407$. Data are from Survey JPN-2.

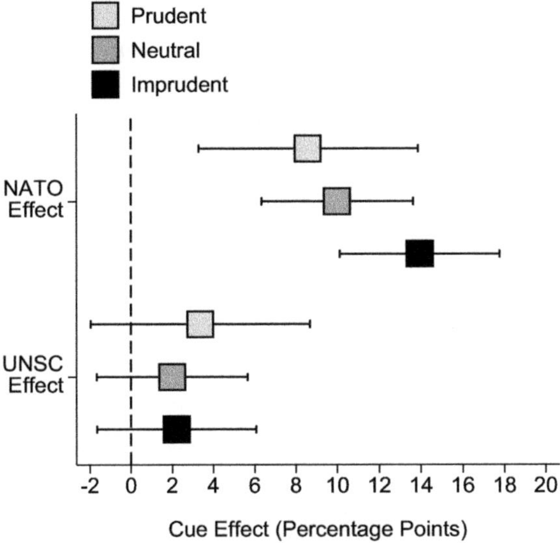

Figure 18 NATO, not the Security Council, reassures skeptics of the United States. This figure shows the percentage point effect of the Security Council and NATO on Japanese approval of U.S. intervention, conditional on whether the survey respondents view the United States as a prudent, neutral, or imprudent military power. $N = 6{,}090$. 95% confidence intervals are given. Data are from Survey JPN1 & 2.

Figure 18 displays the effect of IOs among these groups. Contrary to the reassurance thesis, the more skeptical the audience is of U.S. military power, the more they turn to NATO for political reassurance. Regardless of whether the respondent viewed America as a prudent, neutral, or imprudent military power, the effect of a Security Council cue is about 2–3 pp. In contrast, the impact of NATO grows with the survey respondent's increasing belief that the United States is an irresponsible military power, peaking at 14 pp. among the most skeptical respondents. This trend implies that NATO can play a reassurance role. However, the effect of a NATO cue is about 9 pp. even among those least skeptical of the United States (i.e., those who believe the United States is prudent), implying that NATO's cue is not only about reassuring skeptical audiences.

Material and power-centric perspectives cannot make sense of these findings. If people only held material concerns about unchecked military power in the international system, it would make little sense to seek reassurance from NATO, an organization often associated with a warmongering West. Instead, the social cue theory can demystify these results. Japanese citizens who are skeptical of the United States will look to the liberal community and NATO for reassurance, and even if they do not seek reassurance, they still will respond to social pressures to support the United States when faced with an ingroup cue. To summarize, this section showed how past evidence can be reframed as consistent with the social cue theory, and it further presented new evidence that raises questions about the core assumptions made by existing theories of IOs.

7 Implications

Nearly every humanitarian military intervention since the end of the Cold War has received backing from an international organization – a striking trend in international relations, almost as consistent as the democratic peace.[188] This pattern challenges the Hobbesian view of international anarchy, which holds that institutions are largely ineffective. Instead, it suggests that countries are willing to cooperate on foreign policy through institutions, even when doing so is costly or compromises their policy autonomy. For example, American interventions in Bosnia, Kosovo, and Libya were steeped in controversy over its involvement with institutions like the Security Council and NATO. Meanwhile, in Syria, the absence of institutional approval stymied President Obama's plans for intervention. Yet, to this date, researchers continue to debate why this close relationship between international institutions and humanitarian intervention exists. They argue that institutions help to legitimize intervention, but questions about how to understand this legitimization process remain. This Element provides a breakthrough in the debate while advancing a general social scientific theory of legitimacy and social identity. In this concluding section, I elaborate upon what my theory and findings mean for scholarship and policy.

7.1 Where the Scholarship Now Stands

This Element theorizes a new perspective on how legitimization functions in political behavior, particularly by developing, applying, and testing the social cue theory to understand how international institutions legitimize foreign policy. While international relations scholars have recognized the political relevance of legitimacy since at least the 1960s,[189] the realist view that dominated through the Cold War largely dismissed institutions as mere reflections of power dynamics, either paralyzed like the Security Council or simply reflecting pre-existing geopolitical competition like NATO. However, as the Cold War waned and global cooperation through international institutions expanded, scholars began developing new accounts of why international institutions

[188] Finnemore 2003; Schultz 2003. [189] Inis 1967.

matter. Some of them, particularly those writing from a constructivist approach, returned to the elusive idea of legitimacy and better specified what it means and how it influences politics at the state and system levels.[190] Subsequently, rationalist scholars reframed legitimization as a process in which institutions, due to their institutional design and membership composition, transmit information about how domestic audiences weigh the costs, benefits, and motives behind a country's foreign policy actions.[191] This Element builds upon these insights about legitimacy and how institutions channel their influence through domestic politics while innovating in theory and evidence.

Specifically, this Element elucidates a new causal model of legitimization from the perspectives of social identity and political psychology. The social cue theory explains how political communities and institutions influence group members by exerting ingroup pressure and alleviating social-relational concerns about norms abidance, group behavior, and status and image. Applied to the phenomenon of humanitarian intervention, the argument implies that the liberal community and NATO vis-à-vis their liberal identity influences the citizens and elites of democracies, the primary participants of these human rights operations. The preceding sections substantiated these claims while ruling out alternative explanations relating to burden sharing, NATO's military strength, mass ignorance, and the liberal community's conflation with Western regionalism.

In advancing a new argument on why international institutions matter, this Element also highlights the limitations of existing perspectives rooted in international law and rational information transmission. For example, the Security Council's authority to legalize actions does not substantially shift public opinion in the presence of ingroup cues, even when audiences are informed of relevant international laws.[192] Additionally, the ability of institutions to exert influence does not appear to depend on public perceptions of their independence or conservativeness, nor can their surprising effects be explained by widespread political ignorance. Nonetheless, the social cue theory does build on the established insight that institutions can shape domestic political views, influencing the views of citizens and elites worldwide.

7.1.1 New Insights into Institutions and Behavior

This Element also provides a fresh perspective on other related bodies of research. To begin, it has implications for understanding forum shopping in

[190] Barnett 1997; Finnemore 2003; Hurd 2008.
[191] Voeten 2005; Thompson 2009; Chapman 2011.
[192] These findings about individual-level attitudes do not imply that international law does not matter at other levels of analysis, such as the state or system levels.

international relations. Erik Voeten's classic paper on forum shopping observes that the Security Council has rarely vetoed resolutions regarding military intervention since 1990.[193] This pattern persisted despite members like Russia and China, who generally eschew military interventions, including humanitarian wars. The paper argues that these countries do not simply exercise their veto because interventionist countries have a credible outside option to the Security Council. In the case of humanitarian intervention, the most salient outside option is NATO. But questions remain: for instance, why might NATO be a credible outside option, and is there evidence for its credibility? This Element shows that NATO is a credible outside option that can exert pressure on politics within the Security Council because it can help interventionist countries mobilize domestic and foreign support for intervention.

Next, this Element's findings about NATO suggest a new way to interpret Philip Lipscy's foundational work on institutional change. Lipscy (2017) argues that international institutions change when competing institutions give member states outside options, allowing them to threaten exit if the primary institution does not meet their needs. This Element challenges Lipscy's application of his theory to the Security Council but in a way that ends up supporting his central thesis.[194] Lipscy argues the following:

> [T]he Security Council has been able to draw on the universality of UN membership and representation among the most powerful members of the international system to facilitate [. . .] legitimizing and authorizing the uses of international force [. . .] As sources of legitimacy, limited-membership multilateral security arrangements, such as NATO, are clearly second-best options.[195]

Lipscy then argues that the Security Council has been relatively resistant to change because it lacks viable competitors. In contrast, this study reveals that the Security Council has a credible competitor in legitimizing war: NATO. But this finding does not necessarily refute Lipscy's thesis. Instead, one can argue that the Security Council has, in fact, changed during the period when NATO became a credible outside option. Specifically, as NATO increasingly became involved in multilateral military intervention in the 1990s, the Security Council was pressured to change one of its core institutions: its ability to authorize war under Chapter VII of the UN Charter. The original intention of the UN Charter was to ban international conflict unless there was a threat to international peace and security. Such a threat to international peace and security could only be determined by the Security Council, as per Chapter VII. However, in the post–Cold War era, coinciding with NATO's increasing involvement in military interventions, the Security Council's

[193] Voeten 2001. [194] Lipscy 2017, Chapter 8. [195] Lipscy 2017, 21.

application of Chapter VII increasingly covered *domestic humanitarian* crises, which are neither interstate- nor security-related (as traditionally defined) and furthermore beyond the intentions of the Charter's post–World War II founders. Thus, NATO provided Western governments with a credible outside option that pressured the Security Council to change its application of the Chapter VII institution, which ultimately supports Lipscy's thesis.

This Element also sheds light on how international institutions affect individual behavior. The "behavioral revolution" in international relations ushered in new research agendas,[196] and among them is one seeking to understand how international law might influence domestic norms and understanding of political violence.[197] For example, can information about human rights treaties or the Geneva Conventions reduce people's approval of various types of political or wartime violence? My study can be connected with existing findings in this literature to generate the following more general insight: *international institutions can shape behavior and opinion only insofar as they resonate with people's fundamental identities, norms, and values*. For example, I find that institutions like NATO can influence mass policy preferences when the institutions resonate with the people's social identity. In a similar way, my previous research concluded that international law reduces public support for wartime torture only when its application is consistent with people's commitments to the norm of reciprocity.[198] As Amitav Acharya argues, the spread and influence of international norms only take hold if they fit in with local conditions.[199] In this sense, international institutions screen and then constrain.[200]

Finally, this Element contributes to a broader arc of literature on identity and political behavior in international relations. It demonstrates the promise of merging social psychological and constructivist approaches to identity. While social psychology offers a theoretical approach to understanding how existing identity affects individual-level behavior that is amenable to positivist research methodology, like experiments, constructivism offers deep insight into the origins, change, and political processes that shape identity in the first place. Social identity theory has relatively little to say about how particular identities become robust and focal points for behavior. It provides a skeleton framework, whereas constructivism, in my application of it, puts the meat on the bones. This analogy is apparent in Section 2, which draws primarily from psychological approaches to generate a general theory of social cues, but then relies heavily on constructivist research to apply the theory to the substantive domain of how democracies wage humanitarian wars. The merger of these two intellectual

[196] Hafner-Burton et al. 2017. [197] E.g., Wallace 2013; Hafner-Burton, LeVeck, Victor 2016.
[198] Chu 2019. [199] Acharya 2009. [200] Simmons and Hopkins 2005.

traditions also breaks a dichotomy that is all too common in international relations research: that rationalism, material theories, and positivist and particularly quantitative methodologies go together on the one hand, while constructivism, social and ideational theories, and interpretivist and qualitative methodologies go together on the other hand. This Element crosses this divide, showing that concepts like legitimacy, norms, and other social behavior need not be "rationalized" to be tested in a social scientific framework.

7.1.2 Future Research on Social Cues

Future research should explore whether social cue theory generalizes to other domains (i.e., external validity).[201] This Element already explored several dimensions of generalizability: it drew from multiple samples across various countries and compared experimental and historical data. I suspect that assessing generalizability in terms of outcomes or the dependent variable – for example, people's support for economic assistance or a military ground invasion versus airstrikes – would yield results similar and correlated to the ones reported here. Instead, future work might focus on whether social cueing matters beyond the humanitarian intervention context. For example, could social cues help to change views and behavior regarding public health, the environment, and the global economy?[202] The social cue theory may also be relevant in several areas of comparative politics, such as understanding social mobilization in light of ethnic and other identity politics.

Researchers should also consider innovating theoretically, as fundamental questions remain. For example, which types of ingroup members can exert the most social influence? What if there are conflicting social cues from within the same community? Next, it would also be useful to explore why people sometimes listen to social cues in some cases but other types of cues – legal, expert, and so on – in other cases. Returning to public health and the environment, these are areas in which cues from technical experts might be especially relevant to policy: would social cues be less critical in areas where there is "objective" technical expertise, and if so, why? Lastly, how do people respond to cues from competing or intersecting salient identity groups? We know people maintain multiple identities, but international relations scholars have made relatively less progress in understanding the consequences of multiple and overlapping identities. The Element also does not theorize deeply about delegitimization and the

[201] This discussion of generalizability is loosely informed by Egami and Hartman (2023).

[202] Research on the COVID pandemic explores whether community or religious leaders could help with vaccine campaigns (e.g., Vyborny 2022; Wijesinghe et al. 2022), but it does not necessarily engage with the concept of social cueing. Regarding international economics, see Gray (2009) and Brutger and Li (2022).

role of outgroup cues. Overall, there is still much to explore in understanding when and why social cues work.

7.2 The Liberal Community and Humanitarian War

Beyond advancing theoretical debates, understanding how international institutions legitimize war has significant practical ramifications, especially for governments weighing the role of multilateral institutions in their foreign policy. The trade-offs are complex. Institutions can confer legitimacy, mobilizing domestic and international policy support, but they can also restrict a country's autonomy and decision-making freedom. Some institutions like the Security Council represent a broader range of the international community, but they are prone to gridlock, which could forestall urgent action to alleviate mass human suffering. Because of these trade-offs, it is essential for policymakers to understand which types of institutions yield what types of effects, whether they be social or material, and why.

This Element does not directly address the ethical debates on humanitarian intervention but offers insights relevant to them. Unilateral actions remain widely unpopular, as seen when President Obama scaled back plans for Syrian intervention in 2013 due to a lack of institutional backing. Yet, as this study suggests, governments seeking legitimacy for their actions may not always need Security Council approval. Instead, political endorsements from ingroup peers and institutions, especially within the liberal democratic community, often confers much of the same legitimizing power. For those advocating greater restraint in international politics, this finding may be troubling: governments can sidestep broad multilateral institutions like the UN in favor of institutions within like-minded communities, reshaping the scope of international interventions.

This Element also highlights a broader question for liberal democracies. As authoritarianism rises and democratic norms wane, institutions like NATO face new pressures and critiques from within. Leaders who question the value of these institutions, often for their perceived costs, may overlook their broader role in sustaining public support for foreign policy and maintaining global stability. While the liberal democratic community has stood together for over half a century, its survival is not guaranteed. Norms, identities, and institutions can erode over time, and this erosion would come at a great cost – not only in lost identity and purpose but also in the institutional tools that have proven central in managing international challenges.

References

Abbott, K. W., Snidal, D., 1998. Why States Act through Formal International Organizations. *Journal of Conflict Resolution* 42, 3–32.

Abdelal, R., Herrera, Y. M., Johnston, A. I., McDermott, R. (Eds.), 2009. *Measuring Identity: A Guide for Social Scientists*. Cambridge University Press, Cambridge.

Acharya, A., 2009. *Whose Ideas Matter?: Agency and Power in Asian Regionalism*, 1st ed. Cornell University Press, Ithaca, NY.

Adler, E., 2008. The Spread of Security Communities: Communities of Practice, Self-Restraint, and NATO's Post – Cold War Transformation. *European Journal of International Relations* 14, 195–230.

Adler, E., 1997. Seizing the Middle Ground: Constructivism in World Politics. *European Journal of International Relations* 3, 319–363.

Adler, E., Barnett, M. (Eds.), 1998. *Security Communities*, Cambridge Studies in International Relations. Cambridge University Press, Cambridge.

Akerlof, G. A., Kranton, R. E., 2005. Identity and the Economics of Organizations. *The Journal of Economic Perspectives* 19, 9–32.

Akerlof, G. A., Kranton, R. E., 2000. Economics and Identity. *The Quarterly Journal of Economics* 115, 715–753.

Aldrich, J. H., Gelpi, C., Feaver, P., Reifler, J., Sharp, K. T., 2006. Foreign Policy and the Electoral Connection. *Annual Review of Political Science* 9, 477–502.

Allan, B. B., Vucetic, S., Hopf, T., 2018. The Distribution of Identity and the Future of International Order: China's Hegemonic Prospects. *International Organization* 72, 839–869.

Bailey, M. A., Strezhnev, A., Voeten, E., 2017. Estimating Dynamic State Preferences from United Nations Voting Data. *The Journal of Conflict Resolution* 61, 430–456.

Barnett, M. N., 1997. Bringing in the New World Order: Liberalism, Legitimacy, and the United Nations. *World Politics* 49, 526–551.

Baum, M. A., Potter, P. B. K., 2015. *War and Democratic Constraint: How the Public Influences Foreign Policy*. Princeton University Press, Princeton, NJ.

Bayram, A. B., 2017. Due Deference: Cosmopolitan Social Identity and the Psychology of Legal Obligation in International Politics. *International Organization* 71, S137–S163.

Bayram, A. B., 2015. What Drives Modern Diogenes? Individual Values and Cosmopolitan Allegiance. *European Journal of International Relations* 21, 451–479.

Berger, T. U., 2003. *Cultures of Antimilitarism: National Security in Germany and Japan*. Johns Hopkins University Press, Baltimore, MD.

Berinsky, A. J., 2009. *In Time of War: Understanding American Public Opinion from World War II to Iraq. Chicago Studies in American Politics*. The University of Chicago Press, Chicago, London.

Blair, C. W., Chu, J. A., Schwartz, J. A. 2022. The Two Faces of Opposition to Chemical Weapons: Sincere Versus Insincere Norm-Holders. *Journal of Conflict Resolution* 66(4–5), 677–703.

Bobrow, D. B., 1989. Japan in the World: Opinion from Defeat to Success. *Journal of Conflict Resolution* 33, 571–604.

Brady, H. E., Sniderman, P. M., 1985. Attitude Attribution: A Group Basis for Political Reasoning. *The American Political Science Review* 79, 1061–1078.

Branscombe, N. R., Wann, D. L., 1994. Collective Self-Esteem Consequences of Outgroup Derogation When a Valued Social Identity Is on Trial. *European Journal of Social Psychology* 24, 641–657.

Brewer, M. B., Gardner, W., 1996. Who Is This "We"? Levels of Collective Identity and Self Representations. *Journal of Personality and Social Psychology* 71, 83–93.

Brooks, D. J., Valentino, B. A., 2011. A War of One's Own: Understanding the Gender Gap in Support for War. *The Public Opinion Quarterly* 75, 270–286.

Brutger, R., Li, S., 2022. Institutional Design, Information Transmission, and Public Opinion: Making the Case for Trade. *Journal of Conflict Resolution* 66, 1881–1907.

Bush, S. S., Prather, L., 2018. Who's There? Election Observer Identity and the Local Credibility of Elections. *International Organization* 72, 659–692.

Calvert, R. L., 1985. The Value of Biased Information: A Rational Choice Model of Political Advice. *The Journal of Politics* 47, 530–555.

Caron, D. D., 1993. The Legitimacy of the Collective Authority of the Security Council. *American Journal of International Law* 87, 552–588.

Chapman, T. L., 2011. *Securing Approval: Domestic Politics and Multilateral Authorization for War, Chicago Series on International and Domestic Institutions*. University of Chicago Press, Chicago, IL.

Chapman, T. L., Reiter, D., 2004. The United Nations Security Council and the Rally 'Round the Flag Effect. *The Journal of Conflict Resolution* 48, 886–909.

Checkel, J. T., Katzenstein, P. J., 2009. *European Identity*. Cambridge University Press, Cambridge.

Chivvis, C. S., 2014. *Toppling Qaddafi: Libya and the Limits of Liberal Intervention*. Cambridge University Press, Cambridge.

Choi, D. D., Poertner, M., Sambanis, N., 2022. *Native Bias: Overcoming Discrimination against Immigrants*. Princeton University Press, Princeton, NJ.

Chong, D., 1993. How People Think, Reason, and Feel about Rights and Liberties. *American Journal of Political Science* 37, 867–899.

Chu, J. A., 2019. A Clash of Norms? How Reciprocity and International Humanitarian Law Affect American Opinion on the Treatment of POWs. *Journal of Conflict Resolution* 63, 1140–1164.

Chu, J. A., Ko, J., Liu, A., 2021. Commanding Support: Values and Interests in the Rhetoric of Alliance Politics. *International Interactions* 47, 477–503.

Chu, J. A., Lee, C. A., 2024. Race, Religion, and American Support for Humanitarian Intervention. *Journal of Conflict Resolution* 68, 2076–2100.

Chu, J. A., Recchia, S., 2022. Does Public Opinion Affect the Preferences of Foreign Policy Leaders? Experimental Evidence from the UK Parliament. *The Journal of Politics* 84, 1874–1877.

Claude, I. L., 1967. *The Changing United Nations*. Random House, New York.

Coleman, K. P., 2007. *International Organisations and Peace Enforcement: The Politics of International Legitimacy*. Cambridge University Press, Cambridge.

Crocker, J., Luhtanen, R., 1990. Collective Self-Esteem and Ingroup Bias. *Journal of Personality and Social Psychology* 58, 60–67.

Dellmuth, L., Tallberg, J., 2023. *Legitimacy Politics: Elite Communication and Public Opinion in Global Governance*. Cambridge University Press, Cambridge.

Dellmuth, L. M., Tallberg, J., 2015. The Social Legitimacy of International Organisations: Interest Representation, Institutional Performance, and Confidence Extrapolation in the United Nations. *Review of International Studies* 41, 451–475.

Deutsch, K. W., Burrell, S. A., Kann, R. A. et al., 1957. *Political Community and the North American Area*. Princeton University Press, Princeton, NJ.

Doyle, M. W., 1986. Liberalism and World Politics. *The American Political Science Review* 80, 1151–1169.

Drifte, R., 2000. *Japan's Quest for a Permanent Security Council Seat: A Matter of Pride or Justice?*. Palgrave Macmillan, London.

Duque, M. G., 2018. Recognizing International Status: A Relational Approach. *International Studies Quarterly* 62, 577–592.

Egami, N., Hartman, E., 2023. Elements of External Validity: Framework, Design, and Analysis. *American Political Science Review* 117(3), 1070–1088.

Epstein, J., 2013. Obama's Credibility Conundrum in Syria. *Politico*. Accessed December 20, 2024.

Fang, S., 2008. The Informational Role of International Institutions and Domestic Politics. *American Journal of Political Science* 52, 304–321.

Finnemore, M., 2003. *The Purpose of Intervention: Changing Beliefs about the Use of Force*. Cornell University Press, Ithaca, NY.

Finnemore, M., 1993. International Organizations as Teachers of Norms: The United Nations Educational, Scientific, and Cultural Organization and Science Policy. *International Organization* 47, 565–597.

Finnemore, M., Sikkink, K., 1998. International Norm Dynamics and Political Change. *International Organization* 52, 887–917.

Franck, T. M., 2002. *Recourse to Force: State Action against Threats and Armed Attacks, Hersch Lauterpacht Memorial Lectures*. Cambridge University Press, Cambridge.

Gartner, S. S., 2008. The Multiple Effects of Casualties on Public Support for War: An Experimental Approach. *American Political Science Review* 102, 95–106.

Gelpi, C., Feaver, P. D., Reifler, J., 2009. *Paying the Human Costs of War: American Public Opinion and Casualties in Military Conflicts*. Princeton University Press, Princeton, NJ.

Gershon, R., Fridman, A., 2022. Individuals Prefer to Harm Their Own Group Rather than Help an Opposing Group. *Proceedings of the National Academy of Sciences of the United States of America* 119, 973–1012.

Gheciu, A., 2005. Security Institutions as Agents of Socialization? NATO and the "New Europe." *International Organization* 59, 973–1012.

Goldsmith, B. E., Horiuchi, Y., 2012. In Search of Soft Power: Does Foreign Public Opinion Matter for US Foreign Policy? *World Politics* 64, 555–585.

Goldsmith, B. E., Horiuchi, Y., 2009. Spinning the Globe? U.S. Public Diplomacy and Foreign Public Opinion. *The Journal of Politics* 71, 863–875.

Goodman, R., Jinks, D., 2013. *Socializing States: Promoting Human Rights through International Law*. Oxford University Press, New York.

Gray, J., 2009. International Organization as a Seal of Approval: European Union Accession and Investor Risk. *American Journal of Political Science* 53, 931–949.

Gray, J., Hicks, R. P., 2014. Reputations, Perceptions, and International Economic Agreements. *International Interactions* 40, 325–349.

Grieco, J. M., Gelpi, C., Reifler, J., Feaver, P. D., 2011. Let's Get a Second Opinion: International Institutions and American Public Support for War. *International Studies Quarterly* 55, 563–583.

Guzman, A. (Ed.), 2008. *How International Law Works: A Rational Choice Theory.* Oxford University Press, New York.

Hafner-Burton, E. M., Haggard, S., Lake, D. A., Victor, D. G., 2017. The Behavioral Revolution and International Relations. *International Organization* 71, S1–S31.

Hafner-Burton, E. M., LeVeck, B. L., Victor, D. G., 2016. How Activists Perceive the Utility of International Law. *The Journal of Politics* 78, 167–180.

Hainmueller, J., Mummolo, J., Xu, Y., 2019. How Much Should We Trust Estimates from Multiplicative Interaction Models? Simple Tools to Improve Empirical Practice. *Political Analysis* 27, 163–192.

Hall, W. J., Chapman, M. V., Lee, K. M., et al., 2015. Implicit Racial/Ethnic Bias among Health Care Professionals and Its Influence on Health Care Outcomes: A Systematic Review. *American Journal of Public Health* 105, e60–e76.

Hayes, D., Guardino, M., 2013. *Influence from Abroad: Foreign Voices, the Media, and U.S. Public Opinion.* Cambridge University Press, Cambridge.

Hemmer, C., Katzenstein, P. J., 2002. Why Is There No NATO in Asia? Collective Identity, Regionalism, and the Origins of Multilateralism. *International Organization* 56, 575–607.

Henkin, L., 1999. Kosovo and the Law of "Humanitarian Intervention." *The American Journal of International Law* 93, 824–828.

Herrmann, R. K., 2017. How Attachments to the Nation Shape Beliefs about the World: A Theory of Motivated Reasoning. *International Organization* 71, S61–S84.

Herrmann, R. K., Shannon, V. P., 2001. Defending International Norms: The Role of Obligation, Material Interest, and Perception in Decision Making. *International Organization* 55, 621–654.

Hicks, R., Tingley, D., 2011. Causal Mediation Analysis. *The Stata Journal* 11, 605–619.

Hurd, I., 2008. *After Anarchy: Legitimacy and Power in the United Nations Security Council.* Princeton University Press, Princeton.

Imai, K., Keele, L., Tingely, D., Yamamoto, T., 2011. Unpacking the Black Box of Causality: Learning about Causal Mechanisms from Experimental and Observational Studies. *American Political Science Review* 105(4), 765–789.

Independent International Commission on Kosovo, 2000. *The Kosovo Report: Conflict, International Response, Lessons Learned.* Oxford University Press, New York.

Izumikawa, Y., 2010. Explaining Japanese Antimilitarism: Normative and Realist Constraints on Japan's Security Policy. *International Security* 35, 123–160.

Johns, R., Davies, G. A. M., 2012. Democratic Peace or Clash of Civilizations? Target States and Support for War in Britain and the United States. *The Journal of Politics* 74, 1038–1052.

Johnson, C., 1975. Japan: Who Governs? An Essay on Official Bureaucracy. *Journal of Japanese Studies* 2, 1–28.

Johnston, A. I., 2012. What (If Anything) Does East Asia Tell Us about International Relations Theory? *Annual Review of Political Science* 15, 53–78.

Johnston, A. I., 2008. *Social States: China in International Institutions, 1980–2000*. Princeton University Press, Princeton, NJ.

Johnston, A. I., 2001. Treating International Institutions as Social Environments. *International Studies Quarterly* 45, 487–515.

Katzenstein, P. J., 2008. *Rethinking Japanese Security: Internal and External Dimensions*. Routledge, London.

Katzenstein, P. J., 2009. European Identity. Cambridge University Press, Cambridge.

Katzenstein, P. J., 1996a. *Cultural Norms and National Security: Police and Military in Postwar Japan*. Cornell University Press, Ithaca, NY.

Katzenstein, P. J. (Ed.), 1996b. *The Culture of National Security: Norms and Identity in World Politics*. Columbia University Press, New York.

Keohane, R. O., 1984. *After Hegemony: Cooperation and Discord in the World Political Economy*. Princeton University Press, Princeton, NJ.

Kerry, J., 2013. "Remarks on Syria." Transcript of speech delivered at the U.S. Department of State, Washington, D.C., August 30, 2013. https://2009-2017.state.gov/secretary/remarks/2013/08/213668.htm.

Kertzer, J. D., 2022. Re-assessing Elite-Public Gaps in Political Behavior. *American Journal of Political Science* 66, 539–553.

Kertzer, J. D., 2023. Public Opinion about Foreign Policy. In Huddy, L., Sears, D. O., Levy, J. S., and Jerit, J., (Eds.), *The Oxford Handbook of Political Psychology*, 3rd ed., 447–485. Oxford University Press, New York.

Kertzer, J. D., Holmes, M., LeVeck, B. L., Wayne, C., 2022. Hawkish Biases and Group Decision Making. *International Organization* 76(3), 513–548.

Kertzer, J. D., Zeitzoff, T., 2017. A Bottom-Up Theory of Public Opinion about Foreign Policy. *American Journal of Political Science* 61, 543–558.

Ko, J., 2023. *Popular Nationalism and War*. Oxford University Press, New York.

Ko, J., 2022. Not So Dangerous? Nationalism and Foreign Policy Preference. *International Studies Quarterly* 66, 1–10.

Koh, H. H., 1997. Why Do Nations Obey International Law? *The Yale Law Journal* 106, 2599–2659.

Kranton, R. E., 2016. Identity Economics 2016: Where Do Social Distinctions and Norms Come From? *American Economic Review* 106(5), 405–409.

Krehbiel, K., 1991. *Information and Legislative Organization*. University of Michigan Press, Ann Arbor, MI.

Lacina, B., Lee, C., 2013. Culture Clash or Democratic Peace?: Results of a Survey Experiment on the Effect of Religious Culture and Regime Type on Foreign Policy Opinion Formation. *Foreign Policy Analysis* 9, 143–170.

Lai, B., Reiter, D., 2000. Democracy, Political Similarity, and International Alliances, 1816–1992. *The Journal of Conflict Resolution* 44, 203–227.

Laitin, D. D., 1998. *Identity in Formation: The Russian-Speaking Populations in the Near Abroad*. Cornell Univ. Press, Ithaca, London.

Lin-Greenberg, E., 2021. Soldiers, Pollsters, and International Crises: Public Opinion and the Military's Advice on the Use of Force. *Foreign Policy Analysis* 17, 1–12.

Lipscy, P. Y., 2017. *Renegotiating the World Order: Institutional Change in International Relations*. Cambridge University Press, Cambridge.

Lupia, A., McCubbins, M. D., 1998. *The Democratic Dilemma: Can Citizens Learn What They Need to Know?* Cambridge University Press, Cambridge.

Maoz, Z., Russett, B., 1993. Normative and Structural Causes of Democratic Peace, 1946–1986. *The American Political Science Review* 87, 624–638.

March, J. G., Olsen, J. P., 1998. The Institutional Dynamics of International Political Orders. *International Organization* 52, 943–969.

Martin, L. L., 1993. *Coercive Cooperation: Explaining Multilateral Economic Sanctions*. Princeton University Press, Princeton, NJ.

Masumura, Y., Tago, A., 2023. Micro-foundations of the Quest for Status: Testing Self-Status Perception and the Multilateral Use of Force. *Foreign Policy Analysis* 19, 1–19.

McDermott, R., 2009. Psychological Approaches to Identity: Experimentation and Application, in Abdelal, R., Herrera, Y. M., Johnston, A. I., McDermott, R., (Eds.), *Measuring Identity: A Guide for Social Scientists*, 345–368. Cambridge University Press, Cambridge.

Mercer, J., 1995. Anarchy and Identity. *International Organization* 49, 229–252.

Midford, P., 2011. *Rethinking Japanese Public Opinion and Security: From Pacifism to Realism?* Stanford University Press, Stanford, CA.

Midford, P., 2006. *Japanese Public Opinion and the War on Terrorism: Implications for Japan's Security Strategy.* East-West Center Washington, Washington, DC.

Milner, H. V., Tingley, D., 2016. *Sailing the Water's Edge: The Domestic Politics of American Foreign Policy.* Princeton University Press, Princeton, NJ.

Mueller, J. E., 1973. *War, Presidents, and Public Opinion*. Wiley, New York.

Nye, Joesph S., Jr., 2004. *Soft Power: The Means to Success in World Politics*. Public Affairs, New York.

Obama, B., 2012. Remarks by the President to the White House Press Corps. Transcript of speech delivered at the White House, Washington, D.C., August 20, 2012. https://obamawhitehouse.archives.gov/the-press-office/2012/08/20/remarks-president-white-house-press-corps.

Pape, R. A., 2005. Soft Balancing against the United States. *International Security* 1(30), 7–45.

Pew, 2013, Public Opinion Runs Against Syrian Airstrikes, *Pew Research Center,* available at: https://www.pewresearch.org/politics/2013/09/03/public-opinion-runs-against-syrian-airstrikes/. United Technologies/National Journal. United Technologies/National Journal Congressional Connection Poll: Syria, Sep, 2013.

Politi, E., Gale, J., Roblain, A., Bobowik, M., Green, E. G. T., 2023. Who Is Willing to Help Ukrainian Refugees and Why? The Role of Individual Prosocial Dispositions and Superordinate European Identity. *Journal of Community & Applied Social Psychology* 33, 940–953.

Popkin, S. L., 1994. *The Reasoning Voter: Communication and Persuasion in Presidential Campaigns*, 2nd ed., Univ. of Chicago Press, Chicago, London.

Price, R. M., 1997. *The Chemical Weapons Taboo*. Cornell University Press, Ithaca, NY.

Rathbun, B. C., 2011. *Trust in International Cooperation: International Security Institutions, Domestic Politics and American Multilateralism*, Cambridge Studies in International Relations. Cambridge University Press, Cambridge.

Rathbun, B. C., 2007. Hierarchy and Community at Home and Abroad: Evidence of a Common Structure of Domestic and Foreign Policy Beliefs in American Elites. *Journal of Conflict Resolution* 51, 379–407.

Recchia, S., 2025. *Strategies for Approval: Building Support for Military Intervention at the UN Security Council.* Yale University Press, New Haven, CT.

Recchia, S., 2015. *Reassuring the Reluctant Warriors: U.S. Civil-Military Relations and Multilateral Intervention*. Cornell University Press, Ithaca, NY.

Recchia, S., Chu, J., 2021. Validating Threat: IO Approval and Public Support for Joining Military Counterterrorism Coalitions. *International Studies Quarterly* 65(4), 919–928.

Renshon, J., 2017. *Fighting for Status: Hierarchy and Conflict in World Politics*. Princeton University Press, Princeton, NJ.

Risse, T., 2011. *A Community of Europeans?: Transnational Identities and Public Spheres*. Cornell University Press, Ithaca, NY.

Risse-Kappen, T., 1996. Collective Identity in a Democratic Community: The Case of NATO, in Katzenstein, P. J. (Ed.), *The Culture of National Security: Norms and Identity in World Politics*, 357–399. Columbia University Press, New York.

Risse-Kappen, T., 1995. *Cooperation among Democracies: The European Influence on U.S. Foreign Policy*. Princeton University Press, Princeton, NJ.

Risse-Kappen, T., 1991. Public Opinion, Domestic Structure, and Foreign Policy in Liberal Democracies. *World Politics* 43, 479–512.

Sayle, T. A., 2019. *Enduring Alliance: A History of NATO and the Postwar Global Order*. Cornell University Press, Ithaca, NY.

Schimmelfennig, F., 2003. *The EU, NATO and the Integration of Europe: Rules and Rhetoric*. 1st ed. Cambridge University Press, Cambridge, UK.

Schultz, K. A., 2003. Tying Hands and Washing Hands: The U.S. Congress and Multilateral Humanitarian Intervention, in Drezner, D. W. (Ed.), *Locating the Proper Authorities: The Interaction of Domestic and International Institutions*, 105–142. University of Michigan Press, Ann Arbor, MI.

Shinoda, T., 2007. Becoming More Realistic in the Post-Cold War: Japan's Changing Media and Public Opinion on National Security. *Japanese Journal of Political Science* 8, 171–190.

Simmons, B. A., Hopkins, D. J., 2005. The Constraining Power of International Treaties: Theory and Methods. *American Political Science Review* 99(4), 623–631.

Snyder, J., 1991. *Myths of Empire: Domestic Politics and International Ambition*. Cornell University Press, Ithaca, NY.

Tago, A., 2005. Determinants of Multilateralism in US Use of Force: State of Economy, Election Cycle, and Divided Government. *Journal of Peace Research* 42, 585–604.

Tago, A., Ikeda, M., 2015. An "A" for Effort: Experimental Evidence on UN Security Council Engagement and Support for US Military Action in Japan. *British Journal of Political Science* 45, 391–410.

Tajfel, H., 1981. *Human Groups and Social Categories: Studies in Social Psychology*. Cambridge University Press, Cambridge.

Tajfel, H., 1978. *Differentiation between Social Groups: Studies in the Social Psychology of Intergroup Relations*. European Association of Experimental Social Psychology by Academic Press, London, UK.

Tajfel, H., Turner, J. C., 1986. The Social Identity Theory of Intergroup Behavior, in Worchel, S., Austin, W. G., *Psychology of Intergroup Relations*, 7–24, Nelson-Hall. Chicago IL.

Thies, W. J., 2009. *Why NATO Endures*, 1st ed. Cambridge University Press.

Thompson, A., 2009. *Channels of Power: The UN Security Council and U.S. Statecraft in Iraq*, 1st ed. Cornell University Press, Ithaca, NY.

Tingley, D., Tomz, M., 2012. How Does the UN Security Council Influence Public Opinion? Unpublished manuscript, Stanford University.

Tomz, M., 2008. Reputation and the Effect of International Law on Preferences and Beliefs. Unpublished manuscript. https://tomz.people.stanford.edu/working-papers.

Tomz, M. R., Weeks, J. L. P., 2020. Human Rights and Public Support for War. *The Journal of Politics* 82, 182–194.

Tomz, M. R., Weeks, J. L. P., 2013. Public Opinion and the Democratic Peace. *The American Political Science Review* 107, 849–865.

Tomz, M., Weeks, J. L. P., Yarhi-Milo, K., 2020. Public Opinion and Decisions about Military Force in Democracies. *International Organization* 74, 119–143.

Voeten, E., 2001. Outside Options and the Logic of Security Council Action. *American Political Science Review* 95(4), 845–858.

Voeten, E., 2005. The Political Origins of the UN Security Council's Ability to Legitimize the Use of Force. *International Organization* 59, 527–557.

Vucetic, S., 2011. *The Anglosphere: A Genealogy of a Racialized Identity in International Relations*. Stanford University Press, Stanford, CA.

Vyborny, K., 2022. Persuasion and Public Health: Evidence from an Experiment with Religious Leaders during COVID-19 in Pakistan.

Wallace, G. P. R., 2013. International Law and Public Attitudes Toward Torture: An Experimental Study. *International Organization* 67(1), 105–140

Weber, M., 1978. *Economy and Society: An Outline of Interpretive Sociology*. University of California Press, Berkeley, CA.

Weeks, J. L. P., 2014. *Dictators at War and Peace*. Cornell University Press, Ithaca, NY.

Weeks, J. L., 2008. Autocratic Audience Costs: Regime Type and Signaling Resolve. *International Organization* 62, 35–64.

Wendt, A., 1999. *Social Theory of International Politics*, Cambridge Studies in International Relations. Cambridge University Press, Cambridge.

Wijesinghe, M. S. D., Ariyaratne, V. S., Gunawardana, B. M. I. et al., 2022. Role of Religious Leaders in COVID-19 Prevention: A Community-Level Prevention Model in Sri Lanka. *Journal of Religion and Health* 61, 687–702.

Wittkopf, E. R., 1990. *Faces of Internationalism: Public Opinion and American Foreign Policy.* Duke University Press, Durham, NC.

Zaller, J. R., 1992. *The Nature and Origins of Mass Opinion*. Cambridge Univ. Press, Cambridge.

Acknowledgments

This project represents over a decade of research, supported by the insights and encouragement of many. I can only hope that I've acknowledged all of them here. I thank Kirk Bansak, Matthew Baum, Sarah Bush, Christina Davis, Dean Dulay, Moritz Marbach, Erik Gartzke, Julia Gray, Azusa Katagiri, Josh Kertzer, Risa Kitagawa, Benjamin Laughlin, Melissa Lee, Philip Lipscy, Adam Liu, Megumi Naoi, Phil Potter, Piki Ish-Shalom, Anna Schrimpf, Paul Sniderman, Mike Tierney, Yasuhito Uto, Scott Williamson, Matthew Winters, and Jon Pevehouse, and the two anonymous reviewers at *Cambridge Elements*, for their feedback and support on this project.

I am also grateful for the constructive critiques I received during research seminars and conference panels at Stanford, UC Merced, University of Pennsylvania, Chinese University of Hong Kong, Lee Kuan Yew School of Public Policy, International Studies Association, Harvard Experimental Working Group, Midwestern Political Science Association, American Political Science Association, Peace Science Society for their feedback, Carleton Interventions Workshop, Stanford Juku, and West Coast International Relations of East Asia mini-conference (USC).

The work also benefited from the dedicated research assistance of Liam Hoo, Amy Lee, Andrea Low, Hiro Omatsu, and Arthur Shin.

Much of the data collection owes to generous support and guidance from Stanford's Laboratory for the Study of American Values, Regan Kao at Stanford's East Asian Library, National University of Singapore, and the NSF Graduate Research Fellowship (Grant #DGE-114747). I also thank Mike Tomz and Masaru Kono for supporting my research on Japanese public opinion and the research team at Waseda University for providing exceptional localization and translation work. My thanks also go to Scott Williamson and our contracted professional translators for their assistance in implementing the survey in Egypt.

I am especially indebted to my doctoral committee members at Stanford University – Steve Krasner, Ken Schultz, and Mike Tomz – who supported me without fail, even through the many times I considered abandoning this project. During these challenging periods, Danny Choi, Jiyoung Ko, Erik Lin-Greenberg, and several others mentioned previously also provided crucial encouragement that helped me persevere.

Lastly, I dedicate this research to my parents, Caroline and Art Chu, who gave me a world of opportunity.

Cambridge Elements

International Relations

Series Editors

Editorial Team

About the Series

The Cambridge Elements Series in International Relations publishes original research on key topics in the field. The series includes manuscripts addressing international security, international political economy, international organizations, and international relations.

Cambridge Elements

International Relations

Elements in the Series

The Dual Nature of Multilateral Development Banks: Balancing Development and Financial Logics
Laura Francesca Peitz

Peace in Digital International Relations: Prospects and Limitations
Oliver P. Richmond, Gëzim Visoka and Ioannis Tellidis

Regionalized Governance in the Global South
Brooke Coe and Kathryn Nash

Digital Globalization: Politics, Policy, and a Governance Paradox
Stephen Weymouth

After Hedging: Hard Choices for the Indo-Pacific States Between the US and China
Kai He and Huiyun Feng

IMF Lending: Partisanship, Punishment, and Protest
M. Rodwan Abouharb and Bernhard Reinsberg

Building Pathways to Peace: State–Society Relations and Security Sector Reform
Nadine Ansorg and Sabine Kurtenbach

Drones, Force and Law: European Perspectives
David Hastings Dunn and Nicholas J. Wheeler

The Selection and Tenure of Foreign Ministers Around the World
Hanna Bäck, Alejandro Quiroz Flores and Jan Teorell

Lockean Liberalism in International Relations
Alexandru V. Grigorescu and Claudio J. Katz

Tip-toeing through the Tulips with Congress: How Congressional Attention Constrains Covert Action
Dani Kaufmann Nedal and Madison V. Schramm

Social Cues: How the Liberal Community Legitimizes Humanitarian War
Jonathan A. Chu

A full series listing is available at: www.cambridge.org/EIR

For EU product safety concerns, contact us at Calle de José Abascal, 56–1°, 28003 Madrid, Spain or eugpsr@cambridge.org.

www.ingramcontent.com/pod-product-compliance
Ingram Content Group UK Ltd.
Pitfield, Milton Keynes, MK11 3LW, UK
UKHW022147080726
473066UK00010B/811
9781009557313